I0726830

Dead Inside:
Poems and Essays About Zombies

Dead Inside:
Poems and Essays About Zombies

Edited by Lynn Houston, Jennifer Spiegel,
and Susan Allspaw Pomeroy

Foiled Crown Books, LLC

ISBN: 978-1-944355-03-6

Foiled Crown Books
Newburgh, NY 12550
https://foiledcrownbooks.com
Email: editor@foiledcrownbooks.com

Printed in U.S.A

ACKNOWLEDGMENTS

We would like to thank the readers and editorial staff of the publications where the following literary works first appeared:

Rob Carney's "In the Only Zombie Flick I'll Ever Watch" first appeared in an issue of *Sugar House Review* and in his book *88 Maps* (Lost Horse Press 2015).

Kathy Flann's "How to Survive a Human Attack: A Zombie's Guide to Filling the Emptiness and Moving Forward" was originally published in *Word Riot.*

Mary Jo Firth Gillet's "Zombie Preparedness Plan" was included in an issue of *The Southern Review* and also in a chapbook, *Dance Like a Flame*, which won the Hill-Stead Sunken Garden Poetry Prize in 2013.

Elizabeth Hazen's "Why I Love Zombie Woman #6" first came out in *Gargoyle Magazine.*

Adrian C. Louis' "When I was a Zombie" was originally included in an issue of *South Dakota Review.*

Peter E. Murphy's "Obsessing the Sabbath" is from his chapbook *The Last Pub on Earth* (Five Oaks Press).

Jennifer Perrine's "Portrait of My Lover as Zombie" was included in her collection *In the Human Zoo*, a title put out by the University of Utah Press.

J.D. Smith's "Zombie Requiem" originally appeared in *Crab Orchard Review.*

Jennifer Spiegel's "Slummin' with the Walkers" contains excerpts that previously existed on the website of *The Emprise Review* (June 2010).

Dawn Tefft's poems, "Endless Summer," "Untitled," and "Daryl Dixon," are also in a chapbook of her poetry entitled *The Walking Dead: A Lyric*, published by Finishing Line Press.

CONTENTS

"Rick leaves his room and finds that the lights are flickering in the hallways. There are several overturned beds and papers laying everywhere. Rick shuffles down the hallways. He comes to a desk and picks up the phone, but he is unable to get a dial tone. In one of the bins, he finds a pack of matches. He picks it up and lights one to make sure it works. He continues to walk down the dark hallway and looks through a door. On the other side on the floor is a dead woman that is missing her abdomen and her entrails are hanging out of her stomach. Disgusted, Rick continues down the wall. He sees bullet holes and blood stains on the walls and walks toward a door that says, "Don't open, Dead Inside." When he approaches it, the door starts to push open but the lock and board that was placed on it prevents it from opening. Hands that look pale and dirty reach out to try to get at Rick, but he runs away from it. He tries to get inside the elevator, but it isn't working. He runs into the stairwell, but it is dark inside. He lights several matches and walks down. Rick finally reaches the bottom and goes outside into the light."

~ *The Walking Dead*, script of Season 1, Episode 1 "Days Gone By"

In Defense of Zombies: An Introduction

Lynn Marie Houston, Susan Allspaw Pomeroy, and Jennifer Spiegel

It's easy to dismiss the zombie as a passing trend in popular culture, or bemoan it as a sign of the degradation of our literary and cinematic tastes. And yet. . . the zombie persists.

Zombies don't just pepper the latest editions of *Pride and Prejudice* like a new kid-friendly Wheaties box design. Zombies don't simply lurch down deserted alleyways in Hollywood studio lots. Rather, entire books of poetry are now being published on the topic. As new generations of writers, filmmakers, and artists continue to revisit the notion of the undead and continue to add to the richness of its legacy, we have to ask what fascinates us so much about this particular monster. The authors of the poems and essays in this collection provide robust responses to that question.

The high ratings of AMC's television series *The Walking Dead* is a testament to how fictional apocalyptical imaginations are easily sparked, how zombie-play is effortlessly woven into our narratives. We are eager to talk about what we would shove into our one small knapsack. We can't wait to tell about our plan to stake out Costco or build a moat around Home Depot. We've got it all planned out. First, we'd raid the hospital for antibiotics. Second, we'd definitely carry a lot of matches and beef jerky. We are eager to debate the whereabouts of beloved pets in the zombie apocalypse. Why do we slip so easily into this story?

Is there more to it? On some level, do we share this undead-dead state of being? Coming out of the "heyday" of the 1990s when everything seemed possible after the civil rights era—sexual equality, racial harmony, economic prosperity, and environmental conservation—into the debacle of the 21st Century with its resounding rape culture, its new-old race riots, its terrorist attacks in the name of holiness, its high unemployment, and the many devastating effects of environmental ruin, are we now suffering zombie-like symptoms? Those of us old enough to have lived through this pull of time might feel as if we've been thrust into the savage world of our own zombie narrative, despite persistent electricity and running water. Does the zombie horde now don business suits? Maybe *The Walking Dead* is but a thinly-veiled metaphor for contemporary existence. Many of us feel there is probably little that stands between our lives and those of Rick, Michonne, Daryl, Glenn, Maggie, or Carol. They make a lot of sense to us.

This collection speaks to the tension between our possibly-sick fascination with zombies and our sense of repugnance with their fearful decrepitude. Somewhere within that tension is our continual desire to *know,* to *understand,* to *commiserate* with the post-apocalyptic inhabitants where zombies are the norm. These poems and essays are rich in messages about our frail humanity, messages that transcend overt metaphor. When we decided to put together a collection of zombie literature, it clicked—as quickly as our bonding together to mourn the inevitable death of a beloved character. As writers, we see the richness in approaching our world from the bottom up: from our basest imagination, from the center of disaster. The result is a lens that focuses on our own self-inflicted hunger for something. For what? For what do we hunger? And will we be satiated before the bite comes from behind?

Obsessing the Sabbath

Peter E. Murphy

Garry Morgan wakes covered with rashes
in a restricted area between No Outlet
and Do Not Enter. Another night lying
in the Cardiff underbrush, another week a stranger.
The night before, he shoplifted a candlelit market
darkened by blackouts from the struck mines,
manhandled a small jar, mistaking onion for garlic
powder, dropping it into the deep pit of his overcoat
then cried all the way home.
He is frightened by the closed circuit cameras
that follow him everywhere, even to this park
where a hum of bees camps out in his arms,
his legs, his chest which breaks into hives.
He weeps again when two cardinals fight over carrion.
He is an ache. A howl. If he were a shelf life,
he would expire before reaching the till.
If he were alive he would receive
a telegram telling him he is dead.
Be careful, Garry, or I may have to pull you out.
Garry has developed a selfish allergy:
he wants to become a person who exists.
He chafes and chafes but cannot bleed.
He imagines himself a wild, Celtic warrior,
smiting Edward the First, or a piece of music
that could charm the fleas off a feral cat,
or a dancer who taps into the consciousness
of a fresh keg of bitter ale.
What time do the pubs open today, Garry?
Better get over there early and drink yourself some Brains.

Gettysburg Address

Charles Jensen

These my dead have no souls, our nation is no souled thing these days. Our zombie nightmares of bayonet teeth inscribing their hatred on our necks. Our skin another border to be crossed and crossed out. Before there were states there was a land that bled over itself without boundary. These my dead have no souls. The nation before us had no souls. This green hill before us did not drink blood. These my dead have made it thirst for nothing. This my nation, under God, who cannot bear to watch the slow untangling of America's map. The rivers that carry away this blood now the only breaking points between what is ours and what is our nature. These my dead have no souls. Our nation, wild beast, nipping at its own bound paws.

Zombie Apocalypse Envy Ghazal

Charles Jensen

The zombie movie begins with desolation: everyone's dead.
The main character moves cautiously. His suspicion? Everyone's dead.

And what's so bad, I wonder, envying his solitude, the quiet.
Not a single cell phone or landline is ringing since everyone's dead.

Maybe he'll finally sit down and read *Dune*, or Dostoyevky.
That's what I'd do. Or go on a serious shopping mission. Everyone's dead!

There'd be no lines at Starbucks, not even the DMV.
It's the death of rude employees. All bad service is undone—everyone's dead.

My rent isn't due. No boss owns my time. I'm free!
I'd fill up my Netflix queue, watch films without intermission—everyone's dead.

Sure, I'll eventually get bored. I always do.
But for now, I'm a spectacle, a true limited edition. Everyone's dead!

Everyday would be like Christmas, but only for me.
I'd write myself thank yous. No need to forsake tradition because everyone's dead.

When dinner for one gets too much to bear,
I'll say to myself, *Charlie, go outside. Go get eaten. Join them. Everyone's dead.*

Why the Zombie Apocalypse?

Mac Greene

Zombie
Why not Godzilla? or Martians? Indians or Nazis?
Bomb throwing anarchists or suicidal Al Qaeda?
Why Zombies?

Maybe our fellow travelers on Spaceship Earth,
with midnight fevers and shadows under their eyes,
look like the undead, alive enough to want us dead, too.
Anyone might be the next mass murderer.
Any mother might drown her babies.
Right next door, in the attic or the basement, maybe in plain sight,
there may be a girl who has been captive for a decade,
brutalized by a man who looks like your uncle.
Behind their hipster facades, our neighbors
rot in Denmark and everywhere else.
Zombies push through the floor boards even as we speak.

Apocalypse
A tsunami of living dead abruptly
overwhelms the great system of civilization
The police and the Army abandon their duties
to save themselves, their family and friends.
Everyone instantly becomes victim or survivalist.
Survivalists are suddenly more dangerous than zombies.

Airliners with hundreds of innocents explode
from the sky or crash in the sea.
Children are blown up at their little art shows,
or murdered in a soccer game on the beach.
Girls are tricked and abducted, beaten into sex slaves.
57,000 children walk across the desert to escape assassins at home.
Another boy in a hoodie is killed. Another shooter

arrives at school, or office, or movie theater.
The NRA wants more guns,
even in church, especially in schools.
They want every citizen to be a vigilante.

These are the end of days,
when our neighbors become dead to us,
when fear overwhelms fellowship,
when no one is safe.

Sunday Night

Steffi Shook

"I don't know if I could do that."
I say through the TV glow.
"No need to worry. Not like I'll become a zombie."
But he will.
We'll all be rotting on the sidewalks.
Scrapping at the ankles of the ones who loved us.
Howling in their ears at night.
Saying:
Lay me to rest,
Lock me in the cabinet
So you can live.

Real Friends Shoot You in the Head

Richard K. Weems

In the world of zombie flicks, the slightest level of infection equates to nothing less than the end of the world. Even if the zombie breakout starts on an isolated tropical island, as in Lucio Fulci's *Zombie*, it is only a matter of time before undead shamble along the Brooklyn Bridge.

If you are new to the genre, don't waste your energies grieving for the world. The proliferation of cannibalism isn't the biggest downer of any zombie film. No, the truly depressing moment is the Turning of the Companion, the slow degradation of the movie's trusty sidekick, infected by an ill-fated brush with a ghoul, into mindless flesheater. The Companion can be the witty cohort or the hero's mother, a close chum or a down-on-his-luck boob who is now face-to-face with the grand finale of his galactically bad day. The movie's pathos seeps from the struggle of the dying Companion, who fights with false hope that the strength of willpower alone will somehow defeat the inevitable.

Take for example the fall of Roger, the blond macho SWAT officer from the 1978 *Dawn of the Dead*. Roger, along with his unit compadre Peter, a pregnant news reporter friend and her helicopter pilot beau, take up residence in a shopping mall, which promises to be a perfect place to ride out the end of the world once they banish the zombie mallrats from the premises. But during the cleanout, Roger suffers a bout of tunnel vision, an all-too-common ailment in many horror films. Despite the knowledge that he's surrounded by the undead, he somehow fails to notice the one coming up behind him, who promptly takes a chomp out of his calf as though it were a drumstick.

For the next forty-five minutes of the movie, as Roger writhes in agony, we wince and grimace at his suffering, but don't we really watch in hope that somehow Roger's intestinal fortitude will nullify the zombie virus inside him? Don't we all live under the fantasy that our will alone will offer us reprieve from The End? Even in his final moments, Roger thrashes in his bed and promises Peter he will do all he can to "not become one of those things."

But whether this is our first zombie film or our hundred and first, even in the midst of our hope, we know the Companion is going to Turn. No one overcomes the zombie virus. Even those who flee to safety before the end credits, whether by jeep, boat or helicopter, are usually killed off by the onset of the sequel. Roger dies, and after Peter covers the body with a sheet, he waits across the room—a bottle of Jack Daniel's in one hand, pistol in the other. Eventually, the sheet stirs, and Roger emerges, blue in complexion, his once handsome features sagged into a morose, mindless yawn. Peter, with maybe just a moment's hesitation for his old pal, fires a .44 slug into Roger's skull.

The hopelessness of such situations seems anathema to popular movie culture in general. Don't we go to the movies to be uplifted? But with its seemingly bleak outlook, the zombie genre comes across as the moose-brained football player who grabs the nerdy, soft-hearted rom-com by the ankles and shakes free her lunch money. Zombie movies seem even contrary to the basic tenets of literature. What are works of antiquity like *Gilgamesh* and *Beowulf* about but the strength of men against monsters? Gilgamesh overcomes beasts like the Bull of Heaven and the giant Humbaba, and Beowulf defeats Grendel to form a bond with King Hrothgar of Denmark and forge a lasting peace. Granted, Beowulf and Gilgamesh both die at the ends of their tales, but they meet the inevitable with easy hearts: Gilgamesh with his legacy chiseled into the brick walls of Uruk, Beowulf in a bath of gold and treasure from the dragon he kills in his final adventure. Roger dies a blue-faced liar, and gunning down his SWAT teammate doesn't sit well with Peter—near the end of the movie, he waits for invading zombies with a gun affixed to his own temple.

Even family connections carry no weight when zombies enter the mix. The helicopter pilot in our party of survivors in *Dawn of the Dead* may be his girlfriend's baby daddy, but the second he turns, he leads his fellow zombies to the fake wall that conceals her lair. In the 2004 remake, when Andre's pregnant girlfriend turns, he ties her to a bed in hopes that the child inside her is alive and well. It isn't, of course, and in the end Andre has to gun down both. The virus (not to mention the zombies themselves) in *28 Days Later* is so super-charged that the second a drop of infected blood lands in Frank's eye, he begs the rest of his party of survivors to shoot him in the head, as he knows that he is only minutes away from lunging hungrily at the others, including his own daughter. And in the zombie-movie spoof *Shaun of the Dead*, Shaun has to deal with the turning of both his stepdad and his mum, even though that movie ends on a more positive note and the world assimilates their zombies into society as cart-retrievers in supermarket parking lots and the subjects of reality shows.

***

So is the central lesson of the entire zombie genre that people are not to be trusted, that everyone (friends, family, and lovers alike) will one day turn against us and that we should all seal ourselves up in individual little canisters to avoid all human contact?

No. The above examples remind us that friendship and community are key to our existence and paramount over all else, and that maintaining ties to others is as vital as food or water. Peter's greatest act of friendship for Roger was to wait for Roger to prove he could not keep his promise of holding off the undead impulse and then BLAM! A hole in the forehead, a splatter of brains, and Roger's career in the zombie realm ended in its infancy. The last thing Roger wanted was to lose control of himself, to wander aimlessly looking for flesh he couldn't digest, and Peter obliged. One shot—no more.

In the movies, of course, such metamorphoses are clear-cut and without question. In our mundane existences, however, the problems we need to be saved from are not so easily targeted. Whether we cut ties from one abusive relationship only to fall back into the mitts of another, or decide we would look good with a hipster beard and man bun, or think the pool is an easy jump from the garage roof, or start listening to K-Pop, our poor choices often start with good intentions (in order: he insisted I accept his Find Friends request on our first date because he cares; that guy in the Trivago commercial looked quite fetching; yolo; and GOT7 *really* knows how to dance!) and their destructive ramifications are rarely clear until those ramifications are already reality. In other words, we have a difficult time recognizing our own infections. Thus, we must aspire to be Peters for each other. When our friends turn into monsters, it is our duty to save them against themselves. Yes, we must wait for the right moment, for gunning down our friends before the evidence of their transition is indisputable leads only to arguments and unfriending.

The problem is that our friends rarely turn blue in real life to signal their transformations. Thus, we are left to our instincts, which are often less severe than Peter's.

Take the case of my friend, whom we'll acronym CG. A writer, he dedicated an entire book of love poems to a girlfriend he later found had been cheating on him. Even worse, the book met with some success, and he traveled about, reading night after night from this book that had become a physical reminder of his cuckolding. Upon his return, we met up for an Atlantic City gambling run. After a fortunate run at blackjack, I offered to buy a few rounds at a local watering hole (having grown up in the area, I knew a thing or two about the dives that were off the tourist grid).

The evening started cordial enough. We reviewed our tactics at the craps and card tables, when luck fell our way, when she turned ugly on us. CG found some Frank Sinatra and Tom Waits on the jukebox, to which we crooned and frogged accordingly. I prompted him for war stories from the road, sympathetic for a while to hear about the agonies incurred by his former girlfriend, but by now this tale was a year old, so I prodded him toward a content present. I bought him a cheesesteak. I encouraged him to relish in the pleasures of a successful book of poetry. I didn't let his Coors Light run dry. I tried to show him there were immediate joys to be had.

But CG had rooted himself in a rut of wallowing. He droned on about her cheating heart (luckily, Hank Williams was not to be found on this establishment's jukebox). How she'd borrowed his car some evenings, maybe to see this other guy? How she'd absconded to Woodstock, and how far a drive was that? I nodded the way a bartender does when it's time for you to move on to more sober pastures but offered no further advice.

Then CG got up from his stool and marched off towards the Men's. Needed a moment to himself, I figured, but when he came back, he admitted he'd made a call.

To whom? "Him," he said. "I wanted to know if the bitch ever took my car to see him."

So somewhere around midnight, some guy got a call from a drunk about a girlfriend he'd shtupped a year ago, the drunken bastard's slurs probably made even more unintelligible by the background jukebox as he demanded to know if his ex ever showed up for a screw in a white Toyota.

The answer? CG got nothing that satisfied his gesture, just a bunch of denials and professions of ignorance. For all I knew, CG might not have known this other guy at all and had verbally accosted a stranger whose only crime was to own the number CG had haphazardly punched into the keypad.

But now, I realize CG told me about the conversation the way one threatens self-injury to a hotline operator--as a cry for help. But rather than put my crosshairs on his forehead and chew him out for such a silly, self-flagelatting gesture, I offered him another round as though the man needed consolation as opposed to a confrontation. All too often, the zombie apocalypse starts with those too limp-wristed to gun down those they care for (thus providing the opportunistic Juan in *Juan of the Dead* with his business motto, "We kill your loved ones") and subsequently giving the virus time to proliferate. Over the years, CG devolved from a man devastated over the betrayal of one woman to a man distrustful of just about all of them, in his wake a trail of exploited students and colleagues, systemic philandering, divorce and a son with a rigid visitation schedule.

Could a set of sharp words been enough on that night of drink-and-dialing to stem CG's descent? Hard to say. But at this point, I'm hard put to say they would have done more harm.

***

In the throes of her madness, Ophelia of Shakespeare's *Hamlet* declares, "We know what we are, but know not what we may be." Wise girl. Even knowing who we are can be a challenge, so how are we ever going to know who we will change into over the course of time? We don't have the privilege of living anywhere but in our own skins. At best, we develop a sense of who we hope *not* to become, but even then, how are we to know that we haven't crossed the line into undesired territory?

If we grow up hating everything our mother stands for, how are we to know that we haven't become another version of dear old Mum? That we haven't developed her critical attitudes, her unyielding demeanor?

That's where friends become essential to our sanity and happiness. We often need others to show us when we have changed. Our better friends will be the ones who inform us when that change is not to our liking. Roger would have been mortified to know that he had become "one of those things," despite his resistance, so Peter stopped him immediately, and in the most expedient way possible.

Real friends shoot you in the head—they stop you in your tracks when you've turned down the wrong path.

When I Was a Zombie

Adrian C. Louis

Watching *The Creature from the Black Lagoon*,
the zombies clap when the gill-man
evades the boat's propeller. They raise
Kool Aid in a toast when he escapes
the underwater diver.

Half-fish, the creature only kills to defend
himself. "Those stupid humans caused this,"
says Papa. "What are they afraid of? Can't they
face their own mistakes?" "Yeah," Junior
breaks in. "This human thing is hard.

From the grave to here is a long trip."
Before bed, Junior wrestles with something
his professor said about the truly beautiful
transcending the particular: rosebud, girl's ear,
summer snow capping a mountain. . .

"Shit," he sighs. After all, he's a zombie:
dirt lover, brain connoisseur, dog-tail
worshiper. Never deep enough in the earth
or too far up from dirt is his mantra.

People Who Don't Know They Are Dead

Alan Catlin

> "Multiple personalities, second selves, thought forms, fragments, nature spirits, devas, elementals, the discarnate beings of people who die and do not know they are dead"
> —Gary Leon Hill, *People Who Don't Know They Are Dead*

Card carrying lunatics, UFO abductees,
dimestore drag queens and street corner
preachers saying, *Prepare: The End Is Near*
but there is no end; holocaust deniers, war
mongering profiteers, talkers that say
the street talk, the speaking of tongues
that has no alphabet, no structure, no meaning
outside of the grave; malfeasant drug takers,
sneak thieves and pocket pickers; hot wire car
stealers, white slavers pimping the runaways,
dead enders, bitch slapped adolescents freaked
out and seriously crazy in training bras and
braces; violent psychos newly escaped from
supposedly locked-in wards, walking zombies in
search of the perfect padded room, steal coffins
to wake up in; radioactive experiments gone wrong,
numbers way off the chart and no peaking in sight,
lead suits and concrete shoes to be buried in before
they spread the bad news; translators of the static
between stations making white noise into gibberish,
human speech; brain wave extenders not slowed
by death to the body, life forces slow leaking from
their brains, the study must go even when the subject
has moved from this temporal world to another;
crop circleists and pyramid climbers, mound builders
and henge readers and all their codes, their glyphs,

their indecipherable runes they leave behind;
gravediggers and high priests wielding their shovels
and their swords, their excavations and proclamations,
their poems and their prayers, this living world
and the other, who is dreaming and who is not,
those people who don't know that they are dead
and those people who do.

Papa Zombie, Worried Again About Death

Charles Cantrell

Here
        emerging from my tent
of missing links
        wearing ellipses like
a pearl choker
        bedeviled
by paradoxes lurking
        in my temporal lode
by phrases I glee
        to the guillotine. I am
top heavy with the misleading architecture
        of mercy like when I'd put them
in baggies and drive over them
        with my jacked up Chevy when they
contract dropsy each flapping goldfish body
        popping like a spore in a plastic
bubble sheet. Here
        setting the corner lot on fire
composting epic disasters with
        tainted brush strokes of insomnia
wriggling rascally earthworms in my teeth
        and rivulets of tar on my tongue.
Piffling questions multiply like maggots
        scurrying through the Etch a Sketch
of my mind, atop the skyscrapers in my pockets
        they amplify like a basket of tiny demons
tapping their way out of a baker's dozen of flaming
        eggs. I feel sticky, a bare legged Goldilocks
in a Lazy Boy gallery of toothy Naugahyde, riddle
        of ions in my brain's specks of jelly,
wispy wisps of protoplasm. I can't even.

Zombie Night

Charles Cantrell

When he combs his hair, his scalp
bleeds, pieces of skin fall off. He takes
vitamins and uses a skin cream,
which helps some. Despite his gray skin,
he tried tanning; now he's cream-colored.
His boss, who demands he run the crush-machine right,
(not that he ever runs it wrong, unless
slow for safety is wrong)
calls him a nerd for reading Schopenhauer.
He shouldn't have told him that.
Decadence, decomposition, weakness. . .
they're all the same to him.
He watches piles of metal sway and settle,
flattening violets, black-eyed-Susans,
and buffalo grass near the train tracks.
At lunch the boss said, "There's blood in my stool.
I may have to leave for a week or so,
but I don't give a shit. Get it?" He laughed.
No one laughed, but they got it, and he didn't
give a shit either. He raised his mug. "Here's to your health."
Sometimes he feels like throwing the boss
into the crush machine, see how small
and silvery, with aluminum lips and ears,
he'd come out. To some extent, the boss enslaves his will,
which is, according to Schopenhauer, the root
of most evil. He puts those thoughts away,
smoking in the john (against the rules).
When the boss said, "I thought you'd fallen in,"
he shot the vertical eagle at the back
of his head, then helped fill a truck with blocks
of crushed metal before shift change, and even
with illegal smoke breaks, not a damn minute lost.

What's With My Inner Zombie?

Rikki Santer

A dusty snow in Santa Fe.
In a cracked adobe bungalow
on a nameless backstreet
a pot of beans was boiling.
Not for me I said & ate her
wet brain until arid jellyfish
flew from my eyes. When I
heard her baby cry, I put
on my jacket & booked.
This was during my
no-good years & years
before I would admit
that I had once
been that baby.

How to Survive a Human Attack: A Zombie's Guide to Filling the Emptiness and Moving Forward

K.E. Flann

Humans may look and smell delicious, but don't kid yourself. The statistics are staggering – humans inflict more injuries on zombies than subway platforms or curbs or the tangle of the zombies' own pants. Humans are frenetic. There are those machete beheadings, predictable in their unpredictability. The zombie may also endure gunshots, the loss of a limb to a hard yank, maybe the odd kitchen utensil to the eye.

Zombies have evolved beyond human beings, beyond fear, and yet it's also true that being the object of hatred is exhausting. Have faith. A few simple steps will help you capitalize on your inattention to safety. Maybe you'll bag some brains and come out with both arms attached! Not that you care, exactly. It isn't that zombies are zen, but there's a certain sanguine quality that comes with being undead. You understand that passion exists only in relativity to despair. Still, you'd probably rather have brains and arms than not.

Frequently Asked Question #1: *Loud noise! Brains over there?*

Probably all you will find over there is a beheading. Unlike humans, zombies are not deceitful, so it will never occur to you that you are being tricked. But take heart. Follow these instructions and you will be able to, well, take *hearts*.

When you careen toward the noise, as you will want to do just in case that sound was caused by a cranium, why not knock over some shelves? Humans collect stuff. They think the weight of them will create permanence. When these items topple – items that humans have spent years amassing and more years arranging *just so* onto modular units – you might get lucky. With just the right angle, maybe that Ikea thermofoil wood grain will actually crush someone. Maybe brains will fall out for easy access. But even if you don't crush anyone, the humans will be unnerved to have their permanence dissolved in one swift blow, and you may yet catch a stunned one. You might hear something like, "Oh, not my comic books."

Go toward that.

Frequently Asked Question #2: *Humans use tools. I not. Still want brains.*

Yes, you do. And you can have them.

But it's important to realize that humans will resist with guns, knives, bats, helicopters, flame throwers, lawnmowers, and trained monkeys. As we've discussed, they don't comprehend that death is inevitable. They refer to the future as *the rest of my life*, a phrase they use interchangeably with *forever*. Zombies know that there is no such thing as forever. You exist in a state of desire and hunger, never numb to these feelings, always active, always seeking. No one's going to find you smoking weed and watching *The Voice*.

Humans don't see that by eating their brains, you provide a quick death, more merciful than cancer or liver failure. Instead, they try to avoid contemplating any of it, which would be admirably zombie-like if they could actually do it.

But what can you do? They are who they are.

The main thing to do is to stick together. They can't kill all of you. And you're not afraid to die – you've already done it once. There's really no down side – you will either die and thus be released from the hunger that sears your intestines or you will eat some delicious brains and feel pretty okay for those few minutes. Zombies have a capacity for selflessness and togetherness that humans can't understand. It's all for one and one for all.

The fact that zombies don't sell each other out terrifies humans. As a result, they lose the grip on those machetes, their aim gets shaky, and then they betray each other.

Your tools are purity, truth, and persistence.

Frequently Asked Question #3: *Brains?*

Brains!

Frequently Asked Question #4: *Humans fast. How I bite into skull?*

Humans move so fast that they're blurry. A zombie often can't turn his or her head quickly enough to see them. They're agile, too. Do you remember when you were alive, though? Relative to other animals, humans are the slow ones. And yet, they are near the top of the food chain, eating animals that can outrun or trample them. How? Humans believe they are dominant, and they approach their quarry accordingly, with the steady confidence of the already-victorious. They let panicked animals defeat themselves, and then they flush them into clearings or pens or tractor trailers.

There's a song in *The Lion King* called "The Circle of Life" in which, via animated lions that represent themselves, humans teach their offspring that eating friends from other species is the natural order. But humans are only *near* the top. Zombies are the true top of the food chain. Humans don't like the "Circle of Life" theory when they are the ones staring into the chomping Pacman mouth of that circle.

But that is to be expected. Humans are primitive creatures that are afraid to die and afraid to suffer. Zombies know that life is just a thirty-second dream. Peace and contentment are merely glimpses down that dream's turquoise hallways.

Draw near to your human, the slower the better. The zombie is mortality. The zombie's insatiable hunger is pain. These truths will stun the creature. The more the humans think about death, especially their own deaths, the more panicked they'll get, the more confused – like a bird that bashes against its own reflection. Rip off an ear as you approach or a finger. It is a small price to pay for those brains.

Frequently Asked Question #5: *What is plan-ning?*

Humans throw around phrases like *Organize before they rise or It's never too soon to prepare for the zombie apocalypse.* At core, they are fearful creatures, like rabbits or fish. But rather than own that fear, the way small animals do, humans like to imagine that they can choose to feel its opposite – anger, perhaps, or supreme confidence. They understand that fear is primitive, and they wish to see themselves as advanced. But they do not grasp that fear has no opposite. *Nothing* does not exist in opposition to fear. It can't oppose or complement. It's nothing. But humans aren't capable of feeling nothing. Only something different. And even then, not really. They only pretend to feel something different. *Plan-ning* is a component in this process.

Humans envision things that they do not prefer. They spend hours of time and energy on these *thoughts,* even though it is, as any zombie could tell them, impossible to envision every possible scenario one might not prefer. The voice in a human's head chatters like a squirrel: *What if the zombie crashes through these replacement windows? They were top of the line, and cost six months' salary, and what if none of that matters in the end? What if I've wasted my life having a job and making money, which is, after all, paper? What if the dog won't stop barking and I have to kill it? What if this spot on my hand is skin cancer? Will the undead smell it?* (Um, yes). *What if my wife leaves me for that dreamy zombie-killer in the chaps and bandolier?*

Humans then devote themselves to preventing these things that have not occurred and may never occur – energy that could be spent on eating or walking. Or, heck, on the bizarre things they enjoy like styling the hair on their heads, kissing, or posting reviews on Yelp.

They amass weapons and duct tape and canteens and gas masks. They position themselves on rooftops and inside rain barrels and on rickety canoes, contorting themselves into positions that make their fragile backs ache. There is SO. MUCH. TALKING. They think that that you don't perceive the hiss of hot breath when they speak in low tones, but it is intoxicating. It is the wavy aroma in a Thanksgiving cartoon they might watch, the way it hooks into your nostrils, the clean baked gingerbread of living flesh.

You never *plan* to smell it, which only makes the smell that much sweeter. You'll go toward it. Why wouldn't you?

If the humans may say things like, "We planned for this. We got this," it's a good sign.

People don't say "We got this" unless they doubt they do. It is the battle cry of the *plan-ners,* the people who know, deep down, that the control they seek doesn't exist. Even if they put a hand grenade in your mouth today, something else will come for them tomorrow. Don't worry (not that you would). They don't got this.

Frequently Asked Question #6: *That light is pretty.*

You're right. That light *is* pretty.

Light is a miracle, a prayer, a whisper. So are eyes.

Zombies have a capacity for appreciation of beauty that humans do not. Probably, the humans have set off a flare gun or a fireworks shell in order to distract you, to tilt your gaze toward the heavens. No matter the pain in your belly, the fatigue from dragging your resistant legs, you will stop. You will let your creaking jaw drop. Orange will streak across the stars, an explosion, a sparkling flower of color.

Probably your head is already gone, already on the ground beside you. But maybe, for a few seconds, if you get a lucky roll, your eyes still see.

Portrait of My Lover as Zombie

Jennifer Perrine

As routinely as kicking off blankets
the dead come back with loose bowels
and Monday morning dread.
Eager for coffee and distraction
they talk football and loudly break knuckles.

But late Saturday it was all souls
picnic in the cemetery when the dead
popped up like tattered tulips
through the sod. Wanting more.

More toast, more jelly they say.
More TV. Beer, now, in cold bottles.
More women with long legs.
More women smelling like torn flowers.

They want to lick up the smiles
slurp the sauce off fingers
go in with the teeth
but their gait is unsteady, their aim unsure.

The dead beget dead as routinely as shedding skin
and fall home to wait for Friday.
They split femurs to tongue marrow
and with ripped lips kiss goodnight.

MONDAY

Jamie Sullivan

You come for me with arms outstretched, low moan
sloping from your hopeful mouth, hands that seek
the warmth of gut and blushing skin, wishbone
plucked from my bird-breast. On your tongue, the reek

of all the others you've devoured before,
their lips still kissing some secret chamber
of your slow-blooded remains. There's no war
in you, no want but that of the monster

to hunt until there's no more prey, to eat
without the need for hunger or the dread
of gluttony. I have no hopes to train

away this shambling seduction, this sweet
disease that whispers for you to embed
yourself in me like teeth inside a brain.

Love Will Keep Us Together, Keep Us from Cannibalism

Lynn Marie Houston

My mother never actually punched me in the face on my 40th birthday. Not exactly. She did raise her fist, shake it under my nose, tell me she would hit me if I didn't shut up. Her ruddy face was inches from mine, spraying spit onto my lip. Although my mother did not actually punch me in the face that day, I believe she was capable of it. She'd hit me before, when I was much younger. Since the incident a few years ago, I've been a little cut off from my body's senses—unable to feel much—and at the same time hyper vigilant to violence.

I know what you're thinking. You need to know what I did at 40 years old to make my mom threaten to punch me. You want to know this part of the story so you can judge the situation for yourself, see if I might have deserved it. This was my response, too, replaying over and over what I might have provoked her. Like I did after she punched me in the chest when I was sixteen. Like I did after every time she embarrassed me in front of company by finding some backhanded way to put me down ("Lynn just doesn't seem to have the skills that others girls have with men; it's a good thing she's so talented in other areas." or "Lynn wasn't born with much natural beauty, but I keep telling her she could overcome that with the right makeup techniques"). That I would blame myself when a family member turns on me in violence speaks to the much longer history of abusive dynamics in my relationship with my mother, a long and painful story that I won't go into here. But for those of you who still want to know the details, let me ask you this: what is it you imagine when trying to conjure up some kind of justifiable rationale for why a mother might threaten to punch her grown daughter in the face? What bad behavior could a 40-year-old daughter engage in to somehow warrant this physical abuse as opposed to, say, a sensible conversation between adults?

Since the near-face-punch, I've seen its negative consequences manifest in my life. I notice I'm surprised when older women appreciate me or praise something I've done. I feel intimidated by people physically larger than me. I walk around generally feeling a little bit unsafe. She's my mother, for God's sake. I have a face that even a mother would punch.

My romantic life has suffered. I briefly dated a guy after the incident, another writer, who sensed something troubled me, who thought he was going to fix me, who told me he was going to help me "live more in the body," which is actually talking about the thing, intellectualizing it, instead of doing it. I think it's one of those goals that is jinxed by saying it out loud because the relationship ended after one tedious weekend together, and I felt no better about anything. During that long time period after him when I was single, a dermatologist once grabbed my hand for a clinical examination and I jumped: the touch surprised me because it had been years since anyone had held my hand.

***

There's a show about the apocalypse I watch religiously—*The Walking Dead*—as if it were the home movies of my own childhood and adolescence, because something about the constant anxiety of survival reminds me of living with an emotionally and physically abusive mother. There's a lot of fist violence in the show, of course: characters punching each other; characters punching zombies; even, recently, a character punching a decapitated head. I keep waiting to get to the scene on the television where my mother holds her fist in front of my face. But I remind myself that the show is a fiction, a fantasy—and yet it picks up on so much that is true about my life, so much that is true about surviving abusive relationships.

The writers of AMC's *The Walking Dead* are among many who weave subthemes of abuse into the character development and storyline of an end-of-the world setting. Carol Peletier and Jessie Anderson (the latter of the Alexandria community) are both survivors of domestic abuse from their husbands. The redneck characters Merle and Daryl Dixon probably took face punches from their father; in Season 3's episode "Home," viewers see Daryl's scars from the severe paternal beatings he endured as a young man. At one point in the show, when both Carol and Daryl are out trying to track down the location of Beth after she is taken hostage by the law enforcement officers running the Atlanta hospital, a book falls out of Daryl's bag: *Treating Survivors of Child Abuse: Psychotherapy for the Interrupted Life.*

Additionally, the Greene sisters experience abuse from post-apocalypse survivors: Maggie is held captive and tortured by The Governor, and Beth is abducted and taken to the Atlanta hospital where she is made a slave, regularly beaten, and narrowly escapes being raped. While Maggie recovers psychologically from her abuse, Beth's response is to lash out, meeting violence with violence. When she sinks a pair of scissors into the neck of her abuser, the woman's gun goes off accidentally, killing Beth.

The show repeatedly enacts this moral judgment: characters die if they cannot survive abuse without turning into an abuser. In Seasons 4 and 5, we are introduced to a group of cannibals at Terminus who become monsters after suffering abuse from a large group that came in and took over, raping and pillaging their peaceful community. Once they'd regained the upper hand, they became the abusers themselves, never trusting newcomers again, killing any who came to seek refuge in their facility, eating them. Their motto becomes "You're the butcher, or you're the cattle," which is a very limited binary in epistemological terms. On the wall of the shrine they'd built to those they'd lost, they write "Never again. Never trust. We First, Always." We are given a flashback to one of the bandits they imprisoned, who keeps repeating, "We're the same," meaning that the victims had become the abusers.

In feeding on people, the members of the Terminus group are no better than zombies. It's a false act of moral judgment, a stereotype—to assume that all people who come to their community have bad intentions. But this is the credo of the person who never gets over being a victim—*never again will I put myself in the position to be abused, so therefore I must become the abuser*. The writers of the show have Rick's people put an end to the Terminus cannibals.

It's how it goes in *The Walking Dead*, where the narrative is an affirmation of what it means to be human. In the face of loss, the show asks us to embrace our humanity, to come back from experiences of abuse and immerse ourselves in a fulfilling life of the senses without equating empowerment and strength to acts of violence. It's why the romances between major characters on the show mean so much to viewers: Rick and Laurie, Shane and Laurie, Glenn and Maggie, Rick and Michonne, even the intimacy-without-sex between Daryl and Beth in Season 4. Through romantic love, an immersion in the life of the senses is possible.

Carol, however, skirts the line between violence as necessity for survival and violence for its own sake: in Season 4, she does in Karen and David, who contracted an unknown fatal illness that could have spread through the prison compound, killing everyone. She dispatches the two infected in a brutal manner, stabbing them while they were asleep and then setting fire to their corpses, despite hope for their survival if given proper medical attention. Rick sends Carol away from the group then, to punish her for a killing that seemed more like murder—cruel and unnecessary—even though Carol's motivation was to protect the others, including the children in the group. Viewers of the show are constantly reminded of Carol's status as a victim of domestic abuse because it encourages her to respond in crisis situations with unchecked violence, as if she were lashing out at the ghost of her abusive husband from her past, who can no longer hurt her except in encouraging her to remain in a cycle of violence by, in turn, hurting others.

Carol exists in tension with the character of Morgan, whose philosophies dictate more nonviolent approaches to survival. Morgan, after a kind of conversion, refuses to kill other human beings, but the truth is that he doesn't even like to kill zombies, avoiding that whenever he can. Morgan and Carol work as foils to each other, both of them responding to plot details by moving along a spectrum of violent capabilities. Carol never clearly crosses the line to become the abuser, and Morgan seems to learn, in turn, that he has to kill to protect.

In the latest season, Season 6, Carol begins to develop an aversion to committing violence after a particularly brutal killing spree to escape from the safe house where members of Negan's group have taken them hostage. Carol's capacity for violence has always been at least tangentially connected to survival of herself or her loved ones, instead of being a power display or entertainment. It is because of this that during Season 6 she leaves the Alexandria community, saying she doesn't want to feel love or concern for anyone anymore because doing so requires acts of violence to protect them.

In addition to Carol, there is another victim of domestic abuse in *The Walking Dead*: Jessie Anderson. Jessie dies in Season 6, not because she herself has become an abuser, but seemingly as a judgment against her son, who has become as paranoid, jealous, and malicious as his abusive father was. The young man repeatedly attempts to kill Carl Grimes, ostensibly over a romantic dispute, as both of them were, at one point, interested in the same young woman. However, the young man's continued plots against Carl put the whole group in danger. In the same scene in which Jessie dies, so do both of her sons, an entire family morally polluted by a failure to disengage from the abuse cycle.

***

On my 40th birthday, my mother nearly punched me in the face because she didn't like what I was saying, because I said I wouldn't read any more emails from my Aunt who was fanning the flames after I called out my older male cousin for grabbing my ass at a family function. I'm seeing a therapist to work through it. I often try to escape my feelings by intellectualizing them, so my therapist asks me to check in with myself. She wants me to ask "how do I feel?" a hundred times a day. Sometime over this last decade of my life, I stopped wanting to feel, and now the challenge is to get that capacity back without being overwhelmed by all the things I've refused to feel for so many years. Any one of the hundred times a day I'm supposed to check in with myself, if I dig deep enough, I can always feel a base of fear and anger. I've come to know those feelings like the final flavor a complex wine leaves on my tongue.

This Valentine's Day, I attended a party at which there was an older, overweight woman who annoyed me. Not for any particular reason. I'd just gotten a bad vibe from her the last time I'd met her. And perhaps because she was older and overweight, she reminded me of my mother. While dishes clinked from the buffet laid out on the table, guests chatted pleasantly, and wine bottles were uncorked, I went into myself and did what my therapist had asked me to do: I checked in with my emotions. What was I feeling at that moment? I noticed how taut my body was, how I was leaning away from the woman while she was telling a story about her dog. How did I feel? A familiar feeling surfaced from my gut: fear. Then I noticed that my muscles were tensed up. Why? Because I suspected that at any minute this woman was going to attack me, as my mother often did—maybe not physically attack me, but at least verbally, the way my mother so often did when we had company over. I was waiting for it. After that moment of realization, I relaxed my body, told myself this woman meant me no harm, that she was not my mother, that the rest of the world was not my mother. And I allowed myself to open up to her, to listen to her funny story about bathing her unwilling terrier and the water and suds that flooded her kitchen. When she left the party, she gave me a hug.

This is the kind of social anxiety tale that almost any abuse survivor can tell. Social situations are hard for those of us who have been fighting for our physical survival. In *The Walking Dead,* Sasha has a similar crisis during a cocktail party held in Alexandria. The leader of the Alexandria community, Deanna, insists on a party to welcome Rick's group, but they've been "out in the field" for so long that they aren't used to the creature comforts the Alexandria group enjoys, like electricity, running water, and ample supplies. The atmosphere of the party—glassware, electricity, abundance of food and drink—is particularly overwhelming to Sasha who has been in survival mode after recently suffering the deaths of both her boyfriend and her brother. She is visibly disoriented in the social situation, where she is expected to be cleaned up, dressed in nice clothes, and make small talk while over-indulging in alcohol and rich foods. The disconnect is too great between the survival mode she's been in and the demands of a polite social function. She loses her patience with the other party-goers and screams at them before leaving abruptly. She has come from a place outside the community where she expects to be constantly attacked.

***

Zombies are monsters because they lack the ethical apparatus to prevent them from inflicting their own condition on others; they are victims who turn into abusers creating more victims. The opposite of this dynamic is *The Walking Dead*'s definition of what it means to be truly human, and it is a trait that exists under constant threat of extinction in a post-apocalyptic world. It's why, to maintain the moral balance at the end of Season 6, someone in Rick's group has to be sacrificed: because they murdered members of Negan's group without provocation, even though Rick thought he had enough justification, attacking Negan's group because they were terrorizing The Hilltop and, in exchange, getting food that Rick's group needs to survive.

Unlike human survivors, zombies are incapable of reasoning their way out of killing, just as they are incapable of feeling enough to fall in love. Some zombie shows play with this notion, turning it on its head, just as recent manifestations of the vampire have given us "vegetarian" vampires, those like the Cullens of the *Twilight* universe who can fall in love with humans because they feed off of animals instead. The movie *Warm Bodies* portrays a zombie who gradually regains his intellectual and linguistic capacities, so much that he saves a human woman under attack from the other undead and falls in love with her. He eventually becomes fully human again as the "disease" wears off and they enter into a romance. Being able to love again after suffering violence is what differentiates humans from zombies.

Four years after my last official romantic relationship, I have started dating a guy who doesn't talk about things like how I live in my body. He is just good to me: attentive, considerate, respectful, and kind. Suddenly, food tastes better, and I'm more aware that I have skin, that it feels good when someone else's skin is close to mine. I'm alive to the senses, aware of nipples and necks and lower backs, parts of the body that had gone relatively unnoticed during those four years when I was single, when my body was just something to feed, let sleep, and treat with medicine when sick.

After about five dates, the guy I'm seeing invites me to his place for the first time. He cooks me dinner, serenades me with his guitar, takes me upstairs to his bed covered by sheets fresh from the dryer and makes love to me. This is the honeymoon phase, and I feel like all the time in the world isn't enough to explore the many joys his body has to offer me. In the heat of the moment, I lose myself and bite down on his lower lip hard, harder than I should have, breaking skin, tasting the copper song of his blood. He cries out in pain. He's hurt. I have become a love cannibal.

Later, when we've collapsed onto each other, our bodies humming, I apologize. I don't want us to inflict any kind of pain on each other, not even playfully. He tells me it's okay, that it's good to learn where the limits are so we can pull back from them. He's understanding. He kisses my cheek, my nose, my lips, everywhere there was once the shadow of a fist.

T-Dog, You Don't Want to Head East

Stephen Roger Powers

Once you make it to the coast you will lose
        180 degrees' worth of directions in which to flee,
unless you follow the moonbeam slick of sweat,
        deodorant, and hairspray washed off those who fled
first. A channel of moonlight for fish isn't the same
        as sunlight pulling you out of a cave,
unless the sharks are a risk worth taking. Keep
        in mind sharks were the first pre-historic biters.
If they bite you out there just beyond the reach of walkers
        you'll end up an eater too, circling forever in the deep,
because that's the way the world works now.
        Maybe it's better to run upstairs. At least
you can shove the lamebrains off the balcony who were caught
        spring-break fucking in their rooms when
the world went to shit, and hope
        the ones on the beach don't figure out
how to climb, otherwise you're no better than a geek
        who doesn't know she's in *Scream* trapped on the top
floor in guttural-gore panic behind a balsa-wood bathroom
        door with no way out but through a pencil-box
window. If we're going to talk about reality,
        let's admit that herds of meat
puppets should be staring at their blank, battery-dead
        smartphones. What else would they have been up to
when they turned? And let's admit, beside a dying
        fire, the ocean at night with a moonbeam on it
swells like the skin of a roamer.

Endless Summer

Dawn Tefft

I've been watching that one zombie stagger
across that field of wheat again and again

a herd of zombies in an endless noisy blur
shaking the trunk of the car where I'm hiding

a zombie cocks its head at me inquisitively
so I aim my knife through the fence link

there's a zombie mother and child pounding
to be let out of the shelter for women

should I go to the well when I know
the water is tainted with bloated zombie

do I open the barn door behind which
my sister prepares her teeth for my throat

even the church pews are filled with zombies
turned while praying, wearing church hats

a zombie is swimming under the water
a zombie is hiding behind the rack of condoms

my father is a zombie and so is my baby
there's no place not streaming with zombies

the forests and the towns and the cities

Daryl Dixon

Dawn Tefft

Daryl is drunk and exploding at the farmer's daughter. Moonshine and a talkative young woman who's gone on vacations. These are the catalysts. But the thing that was smoldering underneath is represented by the shack where they've gone to get Beth her first taste of alcohol. Daryl finds himself immersed in the past even in the dead zone of a zombie apocalypse.

Beth is sweet and vulnerable, but also strong in ways that aren't easily measured. She's genuinely interested in who he is, but finds herself falling back on clichés about bad boys, poor people, and hillbillies. Sitting together in a mess like the one he grew up in, even after endangering their lives to get her the very hardest of liquor, she still can't see him.

I find myself perversely cheering him as he both exposes his injuries and taunts her while playing her drinking game. The rules are to say something you've never done. If the other person's done it, they have to drink. If not, you have to drink. His "I've never"s: been outside of Georgia, gone on vacation. And once they've stopped playing the game and he's yelling: relied on anyone for anything.

In these moments, I want good-hearted Beth to really feel shamed by not understanding what it's like to have had to struggle in the ways poor people do. Or in Daryl's case, poor people who've also grown up enduring physical and emotional abuse.

"I never needed a game to get lit before."

What the other characters view as terseness is really much, much more. It's a lack of knowing how to make himself vulnerable. When you already live a life of extreme vulnerability due to class positioning, every day is another episode in a larger battle. The battle was fixed long ago, and it ain't in your favor. To keep going under these conditions requires toughness. When you try to allow yourself to be vulnerable, you feel the mark of the crosshairs. Instant reminder: the only thing that's gotten you this far is your incredible strength.

It's a lack of material. When you don't have the wide range of formal and informal educational opportunities others have—like going on vacations or traveling outside of the place you were born—you feel you have less to talk about. Or at least less that'll be valued.

It's pride, coupled with fear. Pride in your ability to survive difficult circumstances, which requires intelligence, resilience, and strength. Pride in what other people can't even see about you. Fear that there's something wrong with you, something that destined you to these circumstances to begin with. Or that they've damaged you irreparably.

It's a seething resentment about all of this and needing to talk about it, but knowing that the people you're talking to, these people who aren't even conscious of having acquired a certain ease in navigating the world, won't fully get it. And if they do learn in the ways available to them, they won't want to listen repeatedly. No one wants to be reminded that their positive experiences aren't the results of being more deserving.

Even in the environment of this TV show where everyone loses friends and family to horrors on a regular basis now, people are still shaped by their pasts. Daryl seems to have become especially empathetic because of his past experiences of trauma. He still struggles because of them, too. Daryl—resourceful and used to hardship—might be the one the other characters believe will be the last man standing, but every day he still has to wake with the by now internalized fear that he was born to be "inferior" and "damaged." That he is and has always been merely surviving.

Untitled

Dawn Tefft

A zombie forever tries
to get out of a car.

A grandfather clock
lies dead in the road.

Palms repeatedly beat
against windows.

"We have to stop.
You can be out here too long."

Sunlight shines relentless
through trees.

Half a man crawls
through the grass.

As a gift, someone fixes
the gears of a jewelry box.

The ballerina doesn't turn
until later in the quiet.

Slummin' with the Walkers: Going Rick, or Your Real Guide to the Zombie Apocalypse If We're Talking About The One With Daryl

Jennifer Spiegel

I

I know when my love affair began.

I begin writing this on the morning after Super Tuesday in the heart of the Old West, near the frontier, in the dry desert. I will see dirt today, the powdery brown kind. I will see cactus today, some in bloom. I will sweat and my skin will give off heat, a red heat that looks like damage, like fire. My people never made it to Steinbeck's California with its plump and juicy grapes, and my people, un-moneyed, un-Gatsby'd, are now rooted in the barren desert. We are thirsty all the time. Here, it's more like "Breaking Bad" than West Egg, than East Egg. We'll vote in our primary on March 22. Surely, Trump will win the Old West.

Is this the Apocalypse?

Trump aside, I begin today by writing about my love. Trump aside, I begin today by talking about "The Walking Dead." Dismissing the political heat and the physical climate, I turn to TV—*Will I really turn to television? After all that schooling, after all those lofty and expensive degrees?*—and think about the living, the dead, and the meaning of the Apocalypse.

Contrary to what you might be thinking given my opening, I don't really believe that "The Walking Dead" is about politics—though, of course, it is, too. (I don't actually talk about the show till the tenth page.) What I actually think is that "The Walking Dead" is about the meaning of life!

Did I just say that aloud?

I think I did.

II

The other day, I met an old college friend for coffee. Moving through our favorite topics like one moves through the five stages of grief—our ironic artistic careers after unassuming college majors (he's in theater though he majored in math, and I write despite two degrees in politics), our happy/tragic marriages (to other people), our dogs who eat feces (the both of them), who's the craziest of them all (it's not me), this middle-aged bullshit (fuck it)—we landed on the subject of the finale of "The Sopranos" and, apparently, I had crept to the edge of my seat before blathering on and on, sweat glistening my brow. "At first, I *hated* it," I began, almost quivering with thoughts of Tony listening to Journey in that diner. "But then I thought, *wow,* this is the most *brilliant* end *ever—*"

"You *really* love TV," my old college friend interrupted, uninterested, I guess, in hearing why I thought the end was brilliant.

I do! I love TV!

I guess, for my own sake, I need to justify my TV habit, my love affair, which it is. Nightly, when the kids are down, my husband and I—shamelessly—make our way to the big, brown couch in front of the big screen. He brings over his ubiquitous bowl of Frosted Shredded Wheat and raisins (*why, oh, why did I fail to invest in raisins*?). I've got on my purple socks with paw prints on the bottom for traction. We call our shit-eating dog into the room, making sure he's not chasing my beloved cats. And then, then, for one hour only, we watch TV.

It just seems so—I don't know—*gauche*?

I'm going to tell you a little story. It's embarrassing.

I grew up with parents who watched Primetime TV. *Like every night.* My skinny-ass dad pulled out this black goblet from the kitchen cupboard, filled it with ice cream, and settled in for a night with my mom, miscellaneous pets, and the Idiot Box. Reading this now, I'm like, *Oh My God. I turned into my parents.*

As a teenager, I couldn't wait to get my nouveau-independent, brie-eating, book-reading self out of there, straight into the halls of Academia, where I could get on with the scholarly life. Always a dork, I didn't dream of being a supermodel. I dreamt of Nabokov, Roth, Brontë. While I never stopped shaving and I never joined a Kill-Your-Television

Hate Group, I did ban most TV-watching for years, making exceptions here and there.

But, by the new millennium, single-womaned out, I succumbed. There was a brief, dark time in which I watched "The Bachelor"—alone, in my thirties, with my now-dead cats, prior to hitting up e-harmony with a fake name (*Jennifer Jacaranda*). I had thought I was done with self-inflicted psychosis when I had stopped binging-and-purging in the nineties, but apparently not. I got a grip—though months had passed—and I turned it off, with a kiss-my-ass swivel and a clash-bang-boom.

Fuck Reality TV!

TV-tainted, I swore I'd never relapse again.

The rest of that decade is a hazy blur. I know that, somehow or other, I got married to another hater, had kids, read a book by Donna Tartt (seriously, this is all I remember), saw one doctor about removing my varicose veins but didn't follow up, and began—not without a measure of indignity—watching "Lost" with my husband.

But the crazy part is that TV seemed okay now, even among us faux-intellectuals. No one was ashamed anymore. TV was cool. *Forty was the new thirty, and TV was the new novel*? Damn. Getting old wasn't that bad. Was there a TV Renaissance happening? Were we on the brink, with "Lost," of *Literary TV*?

Well, this story ends badly, I'm afraid.

"Lost" had its grand finale—rife with McGuffins, a *Deus ex Machina* or two, and red herrings galore—and *it killed me*, like, religiously. Part of me *died*. I mean, by now, I was already in the throes of pretending I was a real writer—and I wanted "Lost" to work. I wanted it so badly. *I was rooting for those mofos!* I wanted narrative success, not unlike a sinner craving redemption. With each show's offering of clues and with climactic tension building, my hopes were high. My disbelief was so suspended that I was utterly convinced in the whole thing, Dharma Initiative and all.

But it came to a bitter, bitter end. The show's finale was so unbearably lousy, so disappointing, so theoretically unsound, that I turned off the television for another couple of years. My hands still stained with the sin of Bad TV, I was in need of cleansing (not to be dramatic or anything). The TV stayed off.

Till the Renaissance was in full-swing.

III

This renaissance. For us, it was "Mad Men." Well, "The Office," really. (I stand by the superiority of that show forever and ever.) This was the launch of my love affair, the vehicle by which I bring you Walker-Talk.

We had, I think, entered the second decade of marriage, more comfortable with ourselves and with each other. Though "Lost" had been disillusioning, "The Office" was so freakin' sweet and perfect that we shyly decided to dip into drama. I'm really not exaggerating when I say to you that our mouths slowly dropped open in a kind of artistic ecstasy with the beginning credits of "Mad Men" and our lips did not close again till the final credits rolled. Seven and a half—or whatever-the-hell that was—seasons later. Literary TV was alive!

Don Draper Forever!

We did "The Sopranos." We went for oldies like "Six Feet Under." Right now, we're all over "Breaking Bad."

Yo, Bitch.

But, Dear Reader, my standards are, post-"Lost," very, very high. I want my TV to be like my books, and I'm afraid I'm one of those people who takes her books obnoxiously seriously. If I'm going to devote real marriage-time—*I mean, folks, we're talking about my marriage here*—to sitting on my ass and watching television, we're necessarily talking about Art. I really don't want to hear any of that "it's just entertainment" crap. My husband and I need riveting conversation pieces. We need smart narrative structure, demanding ideas, stirring creativity. We can't be passive TV viewers—this didn't appeal to either of us. (He grew up with his own TV demons: *parents, you don't know what you're doing to your kids.*) We must be active in our pursuits—and TV was a pursuit, *not an escape.*

(I still cringe when people say they watch "just" to be entertained. I don't know if this is really indicative of my own flawed character or what: my uptightness, my inability to have fun, or an anxiety disorder of some kind. I might argue, however, that I want my TV to be both literary *and* entertaining. A lack of entertainment is not part of the equation.)

For me, TV-watching would be part of my writing life, part of my artistic endeavors. I wanted my TV character-driven, not plot-centric. I wanted it to sizzle line-by-line. I wanted a kind of writing perfection. Think about the attention to detail in "Mad Men"—from the choking cigarette mushroom clouds to Betty's feminist revolt contrasted with Joan's similar but different feminist revolt. Think about Tony Soprano's tender spot for animals. Think about the thematic worrying over homosexuality and Christianity in "Six Feet Under." Think about the threading together of ordinary but extraordinary elements like a New Mexico setting, a kid with cerebral palsy, and a one-time promising chemist-turned- high school teacher in "Breaking Bad." Lest you think I ignore comedy, do not forget Tina Fey's brazen comedic commentary on race in "30 Rock" or Amy Poehlor's superb timing in "Parks and Recreation." But, really, the thing I wanted most was a redemptive end. For me, it's all about the end.

IV

Yeah, the Redemptive End.

With "Lost," the question that haunted me was this: *Do you think the producers are gonna pull it off*? It's the end that makes everything worthwhile. We marry whom we marry because of our faith in the end. If a relationship ends badly, the whole thing sucks. Come on, be honest: do you speak fondly of that ex-boyfriend who meant so much and then left you for another woman? You do not. Our religious beliefs are founded on the end. Only if Jesus is resurrected. Only if there are a new heavens and new earth. Only if there is both justice and mercy.

The ends do justify the means. They really do.

So here are some pertinent questions that have informed my own TV-viewing: *Is resolution necessary*? *Are unanswered questions or loose ends okay*? *What do I demand from my narrative*?

I demand resolution.

Some theory. Just a little. Don't worry. Theory in the softest way possible. I'm a fiction-writer, after all. (If this section bores you, skim it—don't skip it.)

In a postmodern world in which nothing is sacred, in which meaning is always up for grabs, in which *Truth* is mythology, narrative is inevitably doused in that which we lack: it can only echo our sorrows, either implicitly or explicitly. Once upon a time, characters had epiphanies; happy endings were possible; an "end" could be had. No more. Postmodernity rejects fixed meaning, the glory of happily-ever-after!

Okay, so it is my contention that successful narratives have "redemptive endings." By "redemptive endings," I am *not* suggesting that narratives must end happily. This is a misnomer that needs to be immediately dismissed. "Redemptive endings" are *conclusive endings that affirm meaning*. (One might ask the following question: isn't it presumptuous to assert that a writer knows what the meaning of anything—such as life—is? But then one might follow up with another equally compelling question: Why would anyone read a writer who had nothing to say? That a writer says nothing nicely—artistic merit—is not sufficient. The lack of content or meaning erodes the artistry.)

Check out contemporary fiction. Stories go out like a flame; the narratives are like windblown dandelions—they're lovely, even proud, somehow bleak; the sound they make is a "whiff." When the book is closed, the whiff is swallowed by real-world noise. These whiffs are forgotten. Contemporary fiction can be highly forgettable. Consider this analogy for a story sans redemptive ending: you're taken to the edge of a cliff. That cliff is staggeringly beautiful and thrillingly dangerous and, though it's a treacherous hike, you're barely aware of strain since skilled hands led the way.

Then, you're left there.

You're not pushed; you're not taken to safety.

Rather, you're left on the edge without direction.

You're left for dead!

This is the effect of the whiff, the lack of the redemptive ending. It's like being stranded.

And, to me, that's how the ending of many contemporary narratives feels.

"Lost." Never found. Ha! The joke's on us.

The concept is simple enough: *a redemptive end is conclusive and it affirms meaning*. "Redemptive" does not necessarily have religious connotations. The grand finale isn't inevitably didactic or preachy, happy-go-lucky or warm and fuzzy. Rather, it's meaningful. And, there's a sense of *closure.*

A discussion on the redemptive end begs another question: *what is art?* At the risk of being overly simplistic, consider John Gardner's words in *On Moral Fiction,* in which he equates art with a universal wound in the human condition, which cries out for healing (181). I like this suggestion a lot. First, it implies that art *hurts*. Second, it points out the universality of the hurt. Art is serious because it's human; art is *for* humans—*all of them.*

(I guess, then, I'm implicitly saying that this Literary TV concept means that TV is—or can be—Art.)

One aspect of being human is holding to belief systems and possessing worldviews. Despite this, our fiction (literature and literary TV alike) seems to keep away from topics deemed "too personal" due to their philosophical or spiritual nature. For me, the personal, the spiritual, and the philosophical are the most compelling topics. Aren't these the themes of the great novels?

Wait. More literary theory that I need to impose on TV. Perhaps you remember Frank Kermode's *The Sense of An Ending,* which examines our need for resolution in literature. Like Gardner, Kermode's theorizing is secular. He argues that novels necessarily have resolutions:

> As soon as it speaks, begins to be a novel, it imposes causality and concordance, development, character, a past which matters and a future within certain broad limits determined by the project of the author rather than that of the characters. They have their choices, but the novel has its end. (140)

Traits we discuss in fiction-writing like cause-and-effect, time scheme, and character development *assume* meaning. We string words together in causal relationships. Fiction-writing is meaningful because it pursues *sensical* relationships. Beginnings assume endings. This assumption affirms meaning. Kermode is applicable to TV, of course.

James Joyce articulated the idea of *epiphany*, a secular moment of truth. This moment of clarity or enlightenment ushers in meaningful conclusion. Epiphany paves the way for redemption. I am, as a narrative junkie, interested in hearing about the epiphanies of others. Though Morgan, for instance, can make me crazy, I am nonetheless interested in his epiphanies in the Zombie Apocalypse.

Has contemporary fiction abandoned epiphany? Perhaps epiphany is impossible in postmodernity. When relativism reigns supreme, revelation and illumination are scarce; after all, who's to say what's revelation and what's not?

This *does* seem to be a stumbling block for the redemptive end. How can a conclusion that affirms meaning be advocated within a relativistic milieu? Think about two of my favorite novels: Dostoyevsky's *Crime and Punishment* and Twain's *Adventures of Huckleberry Finn.* Where would these novels be if good wasn't good, and evil wasn't evil, if all were relative? Is racism ever okay—is it relative? Conviction works against relativity; conviction has to do with naming moral absolutes, with determining good and evil. It isn't shy about finger-pointing.

(Think, briefly, how un-relativistic Rick is in "The Walking Dead.")

We're almost done with the theory part. These, then, are the features of the redemptive ending: conclusiveness (as opposed to ambiguity), meaningfulness (as opposed to meaninglessness), epiphany (as opposed to the sound of a "whiff"), and conviction (as opposed to relativity).

And this is what I want from my TV.

Call me crazy.

V

Which finally brings me, in earnest, to "The Walking Dead."

Here we go. I'll begin by frustrating my editors: *We are not dead inside.*

And this show is going to prove it.

I really didn't want to get involved with this zombie rage, to be honest. I think my husband and I were coming off a "Mad Men" high, and we'd turned off a few recommendations (I've made it risky business to recommend shows to me—coming off as a horrible snob). Then, Tim, for whatever reason, said, *We should see what this zombie crap is all about,* and I was, like, *No? Really?* And, visiting from out of town, my sister plugged it wildly. So, well, we put it on. We had Netflix, of course, like proper Americans.

Okay, I'm not kidding: I was hooked after the first episode (though I pretended to Tim that I needed to see a few more shows to think about it). What, exactly, appealed to me *instantly*? Um, well, hem, haw, it was this: if we were going all apocalyptic, we might—at last—arrive on the good old *raison d'être,* the meaning of life. This show dared, from the beginning, to only deal in the big stuff.

I'm sorry: You just can't talk about The End of The World without throwing into question the meaning of life.

That said, as in the Zombie Apocalypse, everything breaks down from here. I'm now going to *Go Rick* on you, Reader. You were sensing law and order, the progression of ideas, but things get crazy at this point. You know how Rick got that beard and seemed to turn nuts on us, like some kind of overgrown changeling? Remember when Rick ripped open the jugular of that biker-thug with his teeth to save Carl from getting raped? (I was, like, *Go Rick! Go!*) Well, at this point in my bit of pseudo-intellectual prose (I have built my career on bits of pseudo-intellectual prose), I will now offer fragments of philosophy, deep-ish thoughts on what-might-be-going on.

I have to Go Rick on you because, quite simply, quite obviously, the show isn't over yet. Will they do it? Will they pull it off where others have failed? Will they achieve narrative success in this Literary TV Renaissance by concluding with a redemptive end? I think this guide, written on the tail end of the sixth season, must address a number of issues: the existential crisis at the show's core, this whole Literary TV nonsense, apocalyptic politics, family matters, the significance of race (which is probably *the* major theme of American narrative), and God.

Let's think about "The Walking Dead." Finally!

VI

We are not dead inside.

But that is the real question at the heart of this story, which is what makes it great, what makes it Art. And that is why I'm watching. Remember John Gardner's universal wound in the human condition? "The Walking Dead" is, of course, all about that universal wound! I'm practically trembling with excitement as I type. What does it mean to be human? Who are we? And where are we going? Wow! Do you see this stuff on "Everybody Loves Raymond"? On "The Cupcake Wars"? I think not! (I don't mean to slam those two shows; I've only seen a few episodes of the former, and more than a few of the latter, which I kinda like.)

The Apocalypse has long been the subject of Art, and it's still just as prominent in contemporary offerings as it was when John wrote "The Book of Revelation" on the island of Patmos. Now, we're flooded with an admixture of apocalyptic and dystopian visions. The veil has been lifted, and we are desolate. Though we might immediately think of Orwell's *1984*, Huxley's *Brave New World*, Golding's *Lord of the Flies* (yes?), and Bradbury's *Fahrenheit 451*, we're still talking about End Times in Cormac McCarthy's *The Road* (2006). Films love the Apocalypse: *Mad Max*, *I Am Legend*, *The Book of Eli*. Dystopian fiction like Collins' *The Hunger Games* is right there, too, in the unhappy ruins of our world. There are reasons for this preoccupation. Our preoccupation with the Apocalypse reflects spiritual anxieties, deepest desires, starkest hopes. We are anxious about our souls, still perplexed about life or no life after death. We crave meaning, a sense of purpose, peace on earth, a kind of love that lasts. We want for those things to be safe. And our hopes reside here. When we are focused on our ultimate reality, we are focused on what's ultimately important. As absurd as a zombie apocalypse might sound, it would probably get things into sharp focus.

Well, then, "The Walking Dead" builds on this preoccupation, this deep-seated anxiety, this need for meaning. The show poses multiple questions: Where is meaning to be found in the Apocalypse? Why is the Apocalypse always so lousy, so fearful—the future inevitably scary and hopeless? Why are our collective visions so dark? And, once one has accepted the contention that we're preoccupied with End Times, we might turn to a secondary question: Why zombies, our favorite apocalyptic creation? (I'm actually not going there in this piece, though one might cynically—I think—point to some thematic significance in the brainlessness and soullessness of zombies.) The appeal of "The Walking Dead" is that it wrestles with the claim made in the title of this anthology: *Are We Really Dead Inside*?

And if so, why?

From what did we die?

You tell me.

In the fifth season of the show, we hit upon a magic moment when Rick, in the company of Daryl and Glenn, reveals the true meaning of the show's title. All along, we've been calling the zombies "Walkers." The zombies are the Walking Dead, right? But Rick redefines it for us, as he discusses what his grandfather who fought in World War Two told him:

> It was dead men who stepped into enemy territory. Every day he woke up, he told himself, "Rest in Peace, and now get up and go to war." And then after a few years of pretending he was dead, he made it out alive. And that's the trick of it, I think. We do what we need to do and then we get to live. But no matter what we find in D.C., I know we'll be okay—because *this is how we survive.* We tell ourselves that we are The Walking Dead. ("Them")

I really love that scene so much, even though the D.C. thing didn't work out. Feel the woundedness in the human condition? Note, *immediately*, the real focus of this show is on the people, not the zombies. Do not ignore, however, that underlying the analysis brought to us by Rick, Crazy Rick, there is hope. Hope in ultimate victory! The Walking Dead make it out of there alive!

This survivor's ethic underlies it all.

Hope!

VII

If this is Literary TV, what kind of literature?

Still Going Rick on you, let's turn to the question of genre.

Well, this show might just be another take on *The Great Gatsby*. I'm not going to push this too far, lest my head explode (Rick is Jay Gatsby?). But maybe, just maybe, this is a reconceptualization of the American Dream, the first conceptualization having gone under the water in which the boats beat on against the Fitzgeraldian current. Isn't part of the wonder of this show found in the idea of wiping the slate clean, starting over, building America anew? What would this world look like? Is the show utopian or dystopian? Are we embroiled in a utopian drama about the New American Dream?

Besides the Great American novel with its good old American Dream/Rugged Individualism/Marlboro Man fantasy, we might also be dabbling in the Southern Gothic genre. Actually, let me re-state that: *we're plunging headlong into the Southern Gothic genre.*

Relevant fact: Robert Kirkman, one of the big guys behind "The Walking Dead" (whose kid is named Peter Parker, by the way), is from Kentucky. Let's just keep in mind that Flannery O'Connor was from Georgia.

In this Southern Gothic narrative, we're oozing in creeping vines over empty shacks, dark woods overrun with thorns, priests with collars askew, the unspoken but screaming presence of race, weird eye contact, mixed motives, sinister intensions, Carol (so Southern Gothic!) and, um, monsters. Isn't "The Walking Dead" actually part-William Faulkner, part Harper Lee?

Before my next bout of writerly schizophrenia, in which I continue Rick-mania on you, leaving behind this genre stuff, I must quote Carol in season five, demonstrating her perfection as the Post-Flannery Southern Gothic Glinda (The Good Witch of the South). Which viewer will ever forget her infamous threat? When Carol gets caught by Sam in the armory of Alexandria, she says she'll make him a batch of cookies. She says, "But you gotta promise me you can keep it secret." Sam says that he has to tell his mom. He tells her everything. Carol, then, delivers her cookie speech:

> You can never tell anyone. Especially your mom. Because if you do, one morning, you'll wake up and you won't be in your bed. . . You'll be outside the walls. Far, far away. Tied to a tree. And you'll scream and scream, because you'll be so afraid. No one will come to help, because no one will hear you. But something will hear you. The monsters will come. . . and you won't be able to run away when they come for you. And they will tear you apart. . . while you're still alive. All while you can still feel it. And then afterwards, no one will ever know what happened to you. Or you can promise not to ever tell anyone what you saw here and then nothing will happen and you'll get cookies. Lots of cookies. I know what I think you should do. ("Forget")

After that, we were never the same. We knew Carol was a badass already—she had proven that earlier—but now we were, um, happily conflicted. Threatening a child? Over the top? Carol's character, in what is surely, a character-driven show, became even more complex. Initially, we were emblazoned by the new-found strength of a once-weak woman. Then, we were intrigued by her fierce nurturing—which included bloodshed, if necessary. Now, this. Hmm. Too much?

But we like it! Southern Gothic Weirdness!

Of course I'd be remiss if I failed to mention that other chic genre, the Graphic Novel. Really, I've got nothing for you—besides the nod to the genre, on which the TV show is based. I read the first book, but stopped there. Not out of disinterest, necessarily. (Though my interest wasn't profound.) I'm just more into the TV show.

Another pathetic admission: TV before the book!

VIII

We hit the political landscape, which is really more about hitting the moral landscape.

Though it's an election year, I'm not really interested in discussing Trump.

Whatever, man.

The funny thing about this section is that I think I changed my mind while writing it.

Originally, I was going to make the argument that "The Walking Dead" was deeply politically conservative (which is not an original argument, incidentally—there's stuff out there on this topic). But, then, looking around maniacally like Rick (but in slow-mo), I found the show to be politically ambiguous, a little inconsistent—probably conservative, though *deeply conservative* might be pushing it.

There are, however, a lot of guns. *Like so many guns. How do we make sense of all the guns?*

But there is also the small government factor, the prized self-protection ethic, the conservative retreat back (?) towards an understanding of homespun values (they're still giving and taking in marriage during the Zombie Apocalypse. . .) What else? Family values!

In "The Walking Dead," one *cannot* trust the government. Wasn't Atlanta supposed to be some kind of safe haven, protected by the National Guard? Don't forget what happened to the Center for Disease Control. Didn't we just hear about the fall of D.C. and the army's involvement? We saw The Governor do the dictatorial thing. And even the good leaders, like Deanna in Alexandria, are suspect.

(We could also discuss Rick's famous declaration: "Let's get one thing straight, this isn't a democracy anymore," in the Season Two finale, "Beside the Dying Fire.")

It seems a little on the conservative side of things.

However, defining *conservative* and *liberal* may be too slippery within this context. Are we discussing political conservatism and liberalism, or moral conservatism and liberalism?

Consider the show's stance on evil—which is a moral issue? I tend to mix and match my own ideologies, so I'll ask you to consider these questions about morality in hodge-podge fashion.

- In moral liberalism, human nature is basically good. In moral conservatism, human nature is inherently flawed. Fallen. Not so hot. Is this a fair assessment? Does "The Walking Dead" implicitly (or explicitly) take a stand on human nature?
- In moral liberalism, the problem of evil is external—or "out there." (Change the culture/society, the individual is transformed.) In moral conservatism, the problem is internal—within. (Change the individual and the world will follow.) How problems are fixed, then, is affected by worldview. What does Rick think? Morgan?

Characters in "The Walking Dead" probably do not offer any consistent moral theory.

Daryl, one might argue, is an exemplary representative of moral liberalism: the so-called redneck with the heart o' gold. *All men and women are basically good.*

One could just as easily argue that the Zombie Apocalypse reveals one's true nature, and that the heart of darkness is, indeed, rather dark. How do we explain Rick's transformation, from law-abiding, perpetually wedding-ring wearing, sheriff-garbed man of the law to that guy who just blew the head off of Primo in, like, two seconds in Season Six, Episode Thirteen ("The Same Boat")? Is this new Rick "the natural man"? How do we explain Michonne showing up on the scene dragging around two mutilated corpses? How do we make sense of Morgan, whose nonviolence stems from his inherently violent nature? Isn't human nature intrinsically evil in this world?

Perhaps Morgan is the real picture of moral conservatism.

Recognizing his own nature, he has actively worked to tame his demons?

But also keep in mind Carol, *precious Carol.* It's easy to dismiss Morgan's political philosophy as untenable (and nonsensical: Don't you sometimes listen to him and think, *WTF*?). Carol gets it, though. She understands human nature. We are essentially evil, so one does what one has to do to keep it sane. It isn't Morgan's all-life-is-precious mantra, and it's not Rick's ruthlessness. Rather, it's Carol; she's the moral compass of the show. Is this inherently conservative?

We're all over the place here.

Well, it's not terribly *cogent,* is it? (There's a grad school word for you.)

Maybe it's a libertarian show.

IX

With the re-constitution of society comes the re-establishment of family. At the heart of survival in "The Walking Dead" is the need for community. I admit that this warm and fuzzy part of the show completely appeals to me and, apparently, it appeals to everyone. When our people gathered in Hershel's farm, didn't we feel almost cozy—except for the minimal protection around the premises that seemed slightly absurd? The prison felt better, didn't it? But what we really liked best of all was this togetherness, our group, our friends. One of the best scenes is when Michonne is reunited with Rick and Carl when the group is splintered after the prison is destroyed. Oh, we wanted them to find each other! And another great scene is when the banished Carol is brought back into the familial fold, and Daryl weeps into her arms like she is both mother and lover. Didn't you just shed tears of joy somewhere outside of Terminus? Oh, love!

Well, lately, things have been getting a little mushy. The marriage of Glenn and Maggie has always been the symbolic centerpiece of this community business. Despite apocalyptic chaos, people still marry, damn it! Though I've heard Cretans suggest that people would be sleeping around like nobody's business in the event of the Zombie Apocalypse, this show actually works against that premise. Even though Glenn had to take the ring off a zombie's finger, he went ahead and gave that ring to his New World bride!

Right now, with Alexandria getting organized or disorganized, more love is in the air. I have to admit that I personally did a happy dance when Rick and Michonne finally got together (and I'm still doing it). Then we had Abraham's sudden need for the real thing with Sasha, and his nasty rejection of Rosita. This guy, who has a way with words, tells Rosita, "When I first met you, I thought you were the last woman on earth. You're not" ("Not Tomorrow Yet"). Chilly.

Bottom line: this re-establishment of family is at the heart of any vision of the future. Family is not obsolete; in fact, it's stronger than ever. Glenn says it best when discussing his unborn child. He tells Abraham, "We're trying to build something, me and her, all of us" ("Knots Untie").

X

I don't think one can fully discuss "The Walking Dead" without thinking about the role of race, especially if one sees the show as part of the Southern Gothic tradition—which is race-haunted.

As with the topic of conservatism, the topic of race (and patriarchy/gender) has been discussed by far more articulate TV viewers than I. My very favorite discussion is by Thaddeus Howze. He writes this compelling essay called "I've Had It With 'The Walking Dead' Over How It Portrays Black Men," arguing that black guys don't make it in the Zombie Apocalypse, unless they're the sniveling or weak types (a category in which even Morgan falls). He says, in his essay, he's done with the show because he's sick of the slew of dead black guys in "The Walking Dead." (You should look this essay up on the Web.)

I admit that, though I want to disagree, I'm not sure I can wholeheartedly. I want to disagree with Howze because I value the show so much and I am just a white girl and I think his analysis of Tyreese, especially, is flawed and I see the show as making unprecedented strides in some ways—*Man, I love Michonne!*—by normalizing *relationships* between diverse people (it's human versus Walker, not black man versus white man), and by showing a young American-Korean guy in a role never before seen. But, really, maybe Howze has a point.

I suspect, though, Howze is a little unfair.

In this guide to the Zombie Apocalypse, the emphasis is on the content of humanity, on what makes us human. While I may sound frightfully white or naïve here, I think the show is more focused on revealing the universality of the human condition—as opposed to revealing the uniqueness of the Black Man. The human condition is what unites us. We are the humans. In this, we are inevitably, permanently, undeniably united.

XI

In this Guide, with our Rick-like roving eyes, we need to mention "The Walking Dead" and religion. What of religion in the Zombie Apocalypse? Is God now dead?

Well, Gabriel sucks and Hershel's dead, but Carol's been talking faith lately.

Hershel kinda rocked, though.

Basically, the show is not really offering a theological stance, though it hovers over theological concerns. In the Zombie Apocalypse, there is soulfulness (humanity) and soullessness (Walkers). This is its biggest religious insistence: *humans are uniquely human.*

The presence of God is not dealt with.

Father Gabriel, an Episcopal priest, is a joke—and I say to Thaddeus Howze, it's not just black guys who are cringing when Gabriel does some kind of whimpering act: *Christians are cringing too.*

Morality is completely divorced from religiosity here; questions of morality are more relevant to the story than questions on theology. In this narrative, there is good and there is evil. As I mentioned earlier and it's worth re-stating: Carol is the show's moral center. Morgan seems to offer up a lot of mumbo-jumbo. Rick can be a little cuckoo. But Carol may be the ideal.

She better not die on us.

XII

So, there you go. Here's your Guide. You're traversing the thorny, rather lush, creepy landscape of the Zombie Apocalypse. In order to make sense of our narrative, we must ponder the reality of hope, the familiarity of the Southern Gothic surroundings, the politics of the land, the necessity of family, the seemingly-inescapable racial tension, and the question of God.

As much as I love Daryl, I will not riot if he dies.

But I might riot if, after all this, after playing with the Big Themes, after tossing up teleological and eschatological questions alike, the show amounts to nothing. If it lacks the redemptive end, I will riot.

Still: I am watching, eagerly, hopeful. Happy to be a participant in this game.

But I really want that redemptive end.

What works? What doesn't?

If everyone dies and the Zombie Apocalypse continues, *failure!*

If Rick dies, *failure*! (Like literature, Literary TV must be character-driven; to travel all this way with one character—who has transformed appropriately and with complexity—only for him to die would be awful. Why travel with a dead man? Unless he learns something about life. . .)

If we never find out the cause of the Zombie Apocalypse, *failure*! (No unexplained events!)

Lots of potential for failure. Basically, I need an explanation for the Zombie Apocalypse. And then I need for it to end. Though I don't want to see it, they can all die except for Rick—who must emerge from the pile of corpses, stagger further into the countryside, and meet up with other bedraggled survivors. Those survivors must band together and they must live. It would be sweetly poetic if he staggers through that landscape holding Judith's hand—Judith, who is now four or five, and his true child even if her real biology remains a mystery—because family is re-defined. (*Writers. End this show when you're on top; end with grace.*)

That said, I'd like it even better if it were Rick, Michonne, Judith, Glenn, Maggie, Glenn and Maggie's baby, Carol, Morgan, and Daryl emerging from the woods. For that crew, I'd let the zombies gobble up the others. I might be swayed on having a favorable outcome for Eugene, Abraham, and Sasha. I'm a little ambivalent about Tara.

Take Carl already.

Writers, there are a few things I'd love for you people to deal with: May we see Disneyland? How about Manhattan? Do I ask too much? Maybe just a zoo? Why don't we ever see cats or dogs?

You know the one thing that really bugs me? It's not the question of toilet paper or tampons. Rather, it's Heath's glasses. Heath, one of our survivors in Alexandria (a black guy!), wears glasses. We're already pretty far into the Zombie Apocalypse, and Heath has shown that he knows how to deal with Walkers. But his glasses. . .

They worry me.

What if they were to break? What then?

In the meantime, I'm with Rick: "I know we'll be okay—because *this is how we survive.*"

An Epilogue

Well, how do we even deal with that?

Season Six ended last night, and I anticipated waking up to a brave new world in which I'd be forced to tweak my essay out of necessity because Daryl would be dead. Rather, I awoke to a Monday of *Walking Dead*-naysayers: the season finale seems to have been an epic failure—according, at least, to social media.

I guess the big question for me isn't *who died*? (Carl.) The question is whether or not the content of my essay still stands. Guess what.

I think it does.

But, well, I feel a little like I felt after U2's *Achtung Baby* was released. I listened, all full of impossible hopes and expectations, to the album—which might've been a cassette—while sitting on an iron-framed single bed in a dorm room in Brooklyn where I was studying in November 1991. While listening, my mind got working: I tried to weave together something significant, something grand.

But I knew it was all over, and I pretended it wasn't.

That's kinda how I feel right now.

On April 2, 2016, *The Los Angeles Times* published an article by Mary McNamara. McNamara points out that the show, moving towards this season, has been like a "'Mad Men' with zombies"—character-driven, even in the midst of its "uber-plot" (Critic's Notebook). But this season saw trickery. She mentions the non-death death of Glenn. (His name was even removed from the credits during the dumpster fiasco.) While McNamara doesn't mention Daryl's shark-jumping antics, I'd suggest that he's escaped death a little too easily more than once—*even though I want him to.* (And herein resides my own narrative-junkie-conundrum: *I want character veracity, but I want my guys to be safe as well. Jump the shark, but don't jump too high.*) McNamera's ultimate point is this:

> Creator Kirkman recently told *Access Hollywood* that even those who have been following the show for all six seasons are about to discover that while they may think they know the rules of the show, they really do not. . . If the audience does not know the rules of an alternative universe narrative after six seasons, then the writers have failed. If the writers decide to change the rules, or reinvent characters, without bothering to create believable story lines to accommodate those shifts, that's not shocking or inventive, it's just lazy and coldly calculated. And for a show like "The Walking Dead," that year after year showcased the complex reactions of human beings under constant duress by creating an apocalypse that is both external and internal, both real and metaphorical, it would also be an absolute shame. ("Critic's Notebook")

Ouch. I think she's right.

If anything, though, it makes me call into question my original premise on the existence of Literary TV or a TV Renaissance. Maybe, despite the grandeur of narrative, television is still enslaved to market demands. And if that's the case, the creators of "The Walking Dead" need to bow down before the Great Cliff Hanger God. And if that's the case, my definition of success (Rick must live, the apocalypse must come to a meaningful end) is secondary to market considerations. So if we are going to play the game—because it's a game now—centered around who died last night in the hands of hottie villain Negan, let's consider the market. They can't kill Glenn. It's unwise to kill the Asian guy who everyone loves. Continuing with this non-PC talk, no black man is dead because the show gets *tons* of criticism about this. Daryl can't die. Too big of a fan-base. A "safe death" would be Carl.

But about last night: I liked the Carol and Morgan thing. I thought it worked! Finally, I understood Carol, though I think she's nuts. And, hey, Morgan moved in appropriately, yes?

Abraham has eclipsed expectations, moving into the inner circle—no longer secondary. Like a boss.

Eugene's done some development on the Character Arc front.

I dug the look in Rick's eyes, how insane he gets. If they kill him, they really fucked up.

Now, about this Negan.

Return with me, for only a minute to that couch on which my husband and I sit together, watching. Last night was *not* fun. Tim was in a pissy mood. (He'd say I was, I'm sure.) Pointing out everything stupid about the show. I mean, he was totally ruining the mood. I think I asked him to shut up.

But what he really didn't like was that Negan, a super-thug, could have at his command this level of organized, armed evildoers. Tim's disbelief was no longer suspended—which, of course, this fiction wholly requires. The weapons would prevent the organization, so says husband. Once this level of evil is achieved, it's over. What good can come of it? Evil has won.

Well, we exchanged words.

Because I disagreed. *Disagree*. Like so much so.

I'm all like, *Hello? Nazis? The Holocaust?*

I don't know. We started getting hyped up. I'm way more vested in the narrative success of the story than he is or ever will be, so I was sweating.

I let him read my interpretation of our "words," and he says I'm misrepresenting him. He is, I think, making the point that the kind of evil Negan seems to represent is coming off as cartoonish, which is sad in light of the measure of depth the show has achieved in other areas. For example, consider that Negan apparently has at his disposal the man- and womanpower to organize a zombie chain-gang and a group large enough to surround Rick's people in the woods in the dark so they can whistle in unison without night-vision goggles like U.S. Army Rangers would use and without fear of zombies. Consider this. What would Negan want with Hilltop or Rick's group? He can't grow his own tomatoes? He needs Hilltop's cucumbers? What does Negan need from Rick? The pretty little houses? Negan is wanting in complexity. But my husband's criticism—this one sounds valid to me—might be premature. Can the writers move away from cartoonish to the complexity of evil?

While Tim agreed with my emphasis on family and community throughout this "Guide," he also felt like I didn't give Daryl a fair shake, recalling his overall character development. Remember how Daryl went from loner, not even staying with the group, to the one who ultimately went to help Carol look for Sophia? Eventually, he took on Merle, his biological brother. And, now, death of reconstituted family hurts him. *He's* the one who feels the loss of Denise—even though you've already moved on.

This is the show's strength: character transformation, as community and family are re-defined.

But here's the deal. The final scene was cheap. They could've accomplished the whole of the finale in fifteen minutes. They're going to have to really develop this Negan-thing to reveal the hypnotic-level of control one can have over others. The show must ultimately delve into the problem of evil!

Let's just sacrifice Carl to the Market Gods this season!

And don't forget: Enid's in the closet!

I'm a woman of faith. Things change. They can come back.

Works Cited

"Beside the Dying Fire." *The Walking Dead.* AMC. Georgia. 18 March 2012. Television.

"Forget." *The Walking Dead.* AMC. Georgia. 8 March 2015. Television.

Gardner, John. *On Moral Fiction.* New York: Basic Books, Inc., 1978.

Kermode, Frank. *The Sense of an Ending: Studies in the Theory of Fiction.* New York: Oxford University Press, 1967.

"Knots Untie." *The Walking Dead.* AMC. Georgia. 28 February 2016. Television.

McNamara, Mary. "Critic's Notebook: The Trouble With 'Walking Dead's' Season 6 And Its OMG Moments: Has The Show Broken Its Own Zombie Code?" *The Los Angeles Times.* 4 April 2016. 6 April 2016. Web.

"Not Tomorrow Yet." *The Walking Dead.* AMC. Georgia. 6 March 2016. Television.

"Them." *The Walking Dead.* AMC. Georgia. 15 February 2015. Television.

Quarantine

Carrie Shipers

We knew the quarantine would be a joke,
that hundreds of infected would slip
through. We knew supplies would soon

run short, that we'd have to guard
our food and water with our lives.
We stockpiled weapons, studied maps

and basic first aid, packed and repacked
the bags we kept beside our doors,
weighing what we really needed

against what we'd like to have.
We knew the government would lie
to keep us calm, so when we heard

the outbreak had been contained,
the survivors taken to an army base
for interviews and observation,

we knew we'd have to save ourselves.
We practiced building fires and going
without sleep, prying open locks

and busting through plate glass.
We practiced what we'd do if someone
we knew knocked on our door,

held out their arms to pull us in for that
last kiss—. We practiced knowing
what we loved could kill us in the night.

The Zombie Horde

Susan Allspaw Pomeroy

Of course, cities
do their best
to accommodate.
Tall buildings
of anonymity

and tiny swaths of parks
police once swept
with riot gear
to empty the homeless

who were seen then
as the police are now—

unseeing and hungry,
their bodies taking up space
that didn't belong to them.

And now
the ones who lived on the streets
still live
somewhere else

and the ones
who ignored them
wander the city
without survival skills
looking for something
not-dead
to eat.

Zombies Don't Need Chemo

Susan Allspaw Pomeroy

The woman wearing yoga pants
and a wig just finished her fourth round
of chemo when the turn seeped through

her neighborhood. It came in the form of
a good will basket of fruits and crackers
and cheese, that even women in chemo

eat (when they can eat) because gifts of food
make other people feel better about cancer.
She ate the crackers, and after the coughing

started, and nothing felt different than post-
chemo sick, and she was an expert now on post-
chemo sick, she lay on the couch and thought

nothing of it.

When she became the new self after the turn,
if zombies could feel relief, she felt relief,
because zombies don't need chemo,

because their bodies don't care about cancer
or breasts or bald heads, or even yoga pants
or gift baskets of fruit and cheese and crackers,

and even though their bodies crave flesh
like her cancer craved flesh,
she does not respond to the irony,

only to the sounds of so many others,
just like her now, walking bodies,
breathing, black tumors of their own making,

the obvious cure hanging on their bones.

A Map of the Brain

Susan Allspaw Pomeroy

If the zombies were to march right up to my door
and demand my brains, I would ask them
if they wanted the part that calculated how long
it would take to reach my kitchen knives, because I have
no guns in the house, and the knives are as logical a choice
as any blunt object in the event that zombies
come to your door and ask for your brains

or if they wanted the part that asked forgiveness
and cried over the death of that little boy, the one I didn't know
but who died as a little boy and changed the world
with his absence, the part that burst open like a hibiscus
for a day on top of Ob Hill and let the world and all its
Pandora into my body

or if they wanted the part that saw the boulders on Moraki
and the depth of the Canyon from the south rim,
the one that refused to focus for hours on the picture
of my baby girl after they lifted her from my belly
like a heavenly host, an unbreathing heavenly host,

or the part that wrote horror stories in high school
about giant birds (but never zombies, especially not
giant zombies), or giant turtles that tried to cause havoc
but ended up in the wood chipper or blown up
(so long as the girl saved everyone in the end).

If the zombies paused to consider hypothalamus
or hippocampus, if my talking gave their heavy breathing
a moment to pause and debate the merit of a temporal lobe
or occipital, the map from which they were lost,
they may understand the roads to cerebellum,
the river across the corpus collosum, and leave
the bitters left whole in my head.

Zombie Dogs Still Bark

Susan Allspaw Pomeroy

At the once-was-a-park
there are no more chases

only slow sway
of bodies
waiting for a scent
of food
walking by

as dogs used to do,
smelling the air for trouble
or danger
or the scent of a human
who was their favorite
coming home from work
to feed and walk them
to the park
to chase pigeons

before the dogs were bitten
and turned
their smell no longer advantage
but competition
to the non-humans

so they bark
to draw the once-was-friends
away from any fresh
flesh

they bark together
two or three

while the silent ones

sneak up on the meal
and take it.

Still part of a pack.

When the Zombie is a Woman

Susan Allspaw Pomeroy

She does not bother
to groan, as the other
zombies, groaning louder,
still silence her

and while she
is as shuffling-
hungry
as they are,

she will be the last
to eat

because even dead
she still
smells
like the second-class

woman
who should wait
for everyone else
to have their fill.

Why I Love Zombie Woman #6

Elizabeth Hazen

Because she's stuck with stiff and stupid legs,
and decomposing skin, but perseveres;
because she sees without eyeballs, she hears
with oozing ears; because her organs, like eggs
dropped from their carton, hit the path with *splats*,
but still she trudges on; because her need
is clear, uncomplicated: she must feed;
because she barely notices the rats
that gnaw her ankles; because she doesn't stop,
even after the hatchet hacks clean through
her reaching arm; because she will pursue
her prey till they have nothing left to chop.
Because when she lies in piles, inside out,
she will not know regret, or shame, or doubt.

Zombie Preparedness Plan

Mary Jo Firth Gillett

My daughter has discussed at length
the safest place to hole up
in the event of an attack.
She takes her living dead seriously,
seriously considering the necessary
accoutrement for survival:
the basement room where we could hold out
the longest, the handy placement
of the baseball bat—how you can
protect yourself yet still maintain distance.
She stresses the availability
of food and water
in case of a long siege.

I used to plan how we'd survive
a tornado. I used to check out
the closest exit in case of fire.
I practiced defensive driving.
And when I taught poetry in schools near
crack houses, I carried pepper spray—
because sometimes there are no words.
Because like my daughter I believed
I could be prepared. But what she's saying is
it comes for you from unseen corners,
arms reaching, eyes red, vacant. Every day
drops of dew shimmer on the spider's web,
every day a scarab or a monarch
who didn't see it coming struggles.

And if Frost's wry "Provide, provide!"
was clear-eyed, how can I say to her sweet face,

let me tell it to you straight—prepare but it will
not be what you expect. There will be no rabid dog,
no alien vessel, no pandemic. There will be
garbled sounds and then the slack mouth.
I stroke her soft cheek and, against all reason, say
we need floodlights and a backup generator.

Ben Didn't Make It

Aurelius Raines II

I am about ten-years-old. My cousin is spending the night and we are laying in my bed which is under the window, which is in a house which is on the west side of Chicago which is on a block during the eighties. I don't want to disparage my old neighborhood but let's say there was a lot of crack. My room is the safest place that I know.

As we slept that night, a man opened my bedroom window. He walked over my bed while I and my cousin were in it. He opened the door to my room and entered the adjacent living room where my mother was watching "*Magnum P.I.*" He grabbed her purse off the exercise bike that was near my door and then let himself out the front door. I slept through all of it.

At that age, I was a consummate skeptic and may not have fully believed the story that I heard early that morning had it not been for one thing: on my sheets, I could make out a single footprint. This man had walked over my bed *while I was sleeping in it*. In my mind, I imagined the man that would have made it. I still imagined, then, that thieves wore masks like the ones in cartoons. His face would have been shadowed.

Not long after, there were bars on my bedroom window. My parents did not have to convince me I was safe. I had surmised that the strength and position of the bars were enough to keep anyone or anything out. It did not occur to me that I would want to leave through that same window.

Sometime later, I was sitting and watching *Night of The Living Dead* with my father. My mother and sisters must have been gone because it was a "Boy's Night" complete with a scary movie in the dark and Guy's Pizza. (If you are reading this, then I should not have to tell you that this is the movie that established the modern zombie and was about a group of people fighting off the undead and each other in a farmhouse. So I won't.)

I watched the zombies surround the house and try and get in as Ben, the leader of the group, and the people on the inside have a harder and harder time keeping them out. The zombies did not get smarter, just more numerous. I identify as every effort to keep them out is thwarted by decisions made out of desperation and duress. (My father had bought an alarm system that he installed himself. They stole that, too.) Every decision that is made to save their lives only brings them one step closer to death. The wooden panels are snatched from the windows and white, cold, dead hands reach, tremble and grasp. Ignorant and murderous hands looking to rend and devour. As Yeats said, *"The center does not hold. Things fall apart."*

At the end of the movie, Ben is shot by those who would have rescued him.

This is when I started my obsession with zombies. That was my life. I was trapped in this house. My room was the place where I made my last stand. The bars were to keep them out and there were never enough bars. They kept coming in and taking things. There was so much about the plight of Ben and his group that resonated with me. One person with limited resources trying to keep out the mindless and flesh-starved masses.

And they were all around me.

The white kids at school who would call me names that would let me know that our relationship was solely defined by race. I would walk the halls and try to imagine how I would defend myself should they all come after me at once.

My father had told me about a similar situation when he was in high school. Some Greasers from the neighborhood had decided to beat up the handful of black students at one of the city's top high schools. The black boys decided to make their stand in the lunchroom. It only had one entry point and they could use the empty milk bottles as projectile weapons. I would imagine them standing there, my skinny, afro-ed, 15-year-old father waiting behind a line of milk bottle crates, a group of Bens waiting for the hordes to come and try and rip the flesh from their bones.

Fast forward 20 years. I am a husband and a father. This heightens my fascination with extreme safety. I know zombies are not real. Yet, at night, I would look out of my window and imagine a horde coming down the street. Shambling and hungry. I think about how I could defend my home. I pretend to be a zombie with my five-year-old and when his eyes get big with excitement and a little fear I say,

"Whenever you see a zombie, Son, shoot it in the head, even if it's a daddy-zombie. It's the best way to protect your mama."

From that moment on, whenever I come at my son stumbling and growling, his eyes narrow, makes a gun with his fingers, and casually pantomimes a shot to my head. I fall to the floor, defeated.

"Thank you, Son!"

While zombies are not real, there are, still, the flesh-eating hordes who are coming to pull the flesh from your bones.

This time they arrive as the bank foreclosing on our home. And, like Ben, I am convinced to the last that I can defend my home. . . that I can save it. When I am not doing that, I am inhaling *World War Z.* I discover "The Walking Dead." I am becoming distressed as I noticed that my life is becoming like the cold, apocalyptic world I am reading. As we would forgo some utilities to make house payments, the house becomes cold and desolate. I am becoming resourceful both materially and emotionally.

I identify with Rick Grimes and his group as they move from place to place and Rick holds on to the dream that he can make home somewhere, and each time, that dream is broken in a bloody, violent way. I cannot shake the feeling that someone is coming for me and that I will have no idea how to stop them. I look out the window as I think, *Ben didn't make it. Rick had to move.*

So I moved.

***

I don't tell my wife that I picked the second floor apartment because it'll be hard for anyone. . . anything. . . to climb up to the second floor. I don't tell the building manager that I'm annoyed about the sturdy back gate being open because it's an obvious and stupid fault in an otherwise perfect defense system. The last tenant left old furniture on the back porch. I throw it out while I am ashamed of the regret that I have about doing it. *I could barricade the back stairs with this.* I could use the lumber to nail the back door shut.

I play a lot of *Left 4 Dead.* I tell my wife that I'm decompressing after a long day at work. In reality, I am sharpening my tactical abilities. I am careful about my weapons and ammo. I ration health packs. I try to create winning strategies for success. When I complete a level in single player mode, I feel like I could stand the worst. Then, when I play survival mode, the game always throws in some monkey wrench, or one of the other players loses it, and the plan falls apart.

Things fall apart; the centre cannot hold...
The best lack all conviction, while the worst
Are full of passionate intensity.

***

Then Syria happens. I hear about the protests and think that they will have their own success over the ghouls that lumber through the night and threaten to rip into their children's throats.

First, there are the protests. Then, there is the governmental backlash. Next, the people drop the signs and pick up the guns. They are no longer under the illusion that they are fighting people. Finally, the government unleashes its wrath and the families face a familiar choice: fight for home or find a new one.

The reality of their apocalypse doesn't really hit home until I see a picture of a multitude of people fleeing the city. It looks like a scene from DeMille's *Ten Commandments*. Instead of towers of sea water, the people walk through a valley created by the rubble of modern buildings shredded by war. The exposed wounds were once rooms encased in solid brick and mortar. The hordes had come with a force against which there was no defense but flight. Other countries see them coming and close their borders. The citizens are afraid some of the refugees may be infected with the madness that they fled. The countries do not realize that the infected already walk among them until Paris happens and infection breaks out inside the walls.

I think of all the times throughout history that men have stood at their doors to see violent hungry mobs coming for them, knowing that there was no reasonable or available defense. This advancing tide of rotting spirits coming to consume them, mindless and blind to humanity's need to triumph.

It is easy for us to sit in classrooms and judge early pilgrims for their witch trials. We have never had to walk through empty streets, looking for food, family, or friends. Afraid some evil would come out of the muck of the blood-and-fat-soaked earth, ready to pull us down into an unmarked grave.

Who wouldn't you kill to protect yourself from the horror of disease and starvation? During the Black Plague of the last millennia, it was reported that fifty percent of the population of Europe died. That would mean that there were entire cities and towns that were nearly deserted, apocalyptic wastelands only inhabited by a few strong individuals who had to survive among those who were dead. Even more nightmarish, the ambulatory dying, with their disfiguring and oozing boils. Their very breath held the promise of horrible death.

This was not popular fiction. They understood what a zombie apocalypse would be like. So did the Africans who survived in villages robbed of men and women, the Jews who hid in basements while the boots of the walking dead roamed through their breeched homes to carry them away. The Rwandans who covered the mouths and eyes of their children as neighbors ran from house to house, blood soaked machetes in hand. Roman Christians who covered themselves in red gore so they could walk among those who, if they knew about their hidden faith, would consume them. The woman who watched the Khan's army come toward her village in a cloud of death, and knew her only options were rape or death.

For these people, every horror of the imagination was realized and vital.

With all this in mind, my home seems safe, the streets clear and secure. My doors and walls solid enough. My worries seem small and insignificant. The movies, books, games, t-shirts, and social events seem like harmless fun, not warnings.

Yet, I see a cop shoot an unarmed boy on television and I think. . .

And what rough beast, its hour come round at last,
Slouches towards Bethlehem to be born?

Zombie Requiem

J.D. Smith

By the time you read this, the meme
will be going into remission.

Movies will be about Vikings or Ostrogoths,
if not Mongol hordes, time travel,
something that would allow
forbidden love, which does well in focus groups
and saves on special effects
as flesh stays on the bone.
Costume partygoers will no longer
sleepwalk in tattered clothes and intone,
with feigned hunger, *BRAINS*.
Other meanings will slough away,
leaving only Haitian legend and a tiki drink
until the undead's next slow lap
around the culture.

Or this time the undead might be
gone for good, as if the living
had aimed for their heads
and made every shot count.
Their loose, entombed flesh
might at last be found moldering
in the footnote to a history
written for a time of higher seas
and fewer species, observing
the quaintness of an age
that had to embellish its fears.

In the Only Zombie Flick I'll Watch,

Rob Carney

Processional

it isn't brains they're after.
It's our phones—

our iPhones and smart phones,
all our zillion juicy jpgs—

so when the splatter starts,
blood won't geyser onto lawns, intestines

won't tangle in a rose bush.
There won't be cinematic, slo-mo close-ups of wet red

dripping from the leaves.
No bone-cracks splintered by surround sound

or eyeballs popping like gory corks,
just mangled metal, plastic bits, and naked wire. . .

phones stalked and surrounded
and screaming on the swung ends of charger cords

again, and again, and again
against brick walls.

Hold on to your catharsis, people,
the zombies are coming to eat you where it hurts,

Arrival

though of course this is metaphor.
It says so on every syllabus.

It's generic Defense of the Genre 101:
our anxieties projected,

the dead-alive virus of consumerism,
suburban fear of wild animals

whose wildness is safely on TV,
and so on, and so on. Take your pick.

I'm picking Righteous Havoc;
in *The Only Zombie Flick I'll Watch*, they're here

to lash back: Genetically-modified watermelons
made square for easier stacking? Attack!

Mountain Dew ad men asking,
"Are you dissatisfied with your morning-beverage options?"—

slug down another mug of coffee,
blend a pomegranate smoothie,

drink a glass of ordinary orange juice,
and attack! Reach into their servers

and rip out the heart, or chip,
or whatever you call it. Attack.

Burial

Don't worry, they're actors.
And they'd probably all prefer a different role.

One played a genie in an indie film. . .
aired April 8th on the Sundance Channel, 4 a.m.

It didn't pay, but she liked the writing,
liked the wishes of the boy who found her:

"First, turn the guns into hunting falcons.
Then all the bullets into pheasants.

And third, let nobody use this wish
so they can't make any mistakes with it."

When they'd wrapped, after they'd struck the set,
the cast and crew went for Udon noodles,

and the view of the harbor out the window
never looked so clean.

Even now, typecast as a Zombie Prom Queen
grinding her tiara in a redneck's bluetooth,

there's an unspent wish inside her
safe from idiocy and greed.

Recessional

So we've come to the dénouement,
where the zombies are bored with their mayhem.

A few stragglers chase a blonde
in a storm-soaked nightgown,

another gnaws on an iPad,
but they're done. The spirit's gone out of it,

and they lack an articulate spokesman,
a leader to formulate a slogan

they can text
or silkscreen on T-shirts,

maybe hang around wearing them at concerts or something
and stream the whole thing live.

Yeah, that would be easier.
Go home and watch it all on YouTube.

Sit there staring at the new tribal fire
while the final credits roll.

CONTRIBUTORS

Charles Cantrell retired from teaching English at Madison (WI) College in 2005. He has published two chapbooks: *Cicatrix* and *Greatest Hits* 1978-2003. His poems have appeared in over 200 journals, including *Poetry Northwest, The Literary Review, Prairie Schooner, Southern Poetry Review*, and most recently in *Confrontation, Soundings East, UCity Review, Free State Review, Mudfish* and others. His work has been nominated twice for a Pushcart Prize. His awards include several fellowships from Ragdale and the Virginia Center for the Creative Arts, and the 2011 Aga Shahid Ali Scholarship from the Fine Arts Work Center in Provincetown. A full-length manuscript was a semi-finalist in the 2016 Pollak and Brittingham Poetry Awards from the University of Wisconsin Press.

Rob Carney is the author of four books and three chapbooks of poems, most recently *88 Maps* (Lost Horse Press 2015). He won the 2013 Terrain.org Poetry Prize and received the 2014 Robinson Jeffers/Tor House Foundation Award for Poetry. His work has appeared in over a hundred journals, as well as the Norton anthology *Flash Fiction Forward* (2006). He lives in Salt Lake City.

Alan Catlin is a widely published poet. His most recent books are *American Odyssey* from Future Cycle Press and *Last Man Standing* from Lummox Press. He is the poetry editor of the online journal misfitmagazine.net.

Kathy Flann's fiction has appeared in *Shenandoah, The North American Review, The Michigan Quarterly Review, New Stories from the South*, and other publications. A short story collection, *Get a Grip*, won the George Garrett Award and was released by Texas Review Press. It was named a top book of 2015 by *Baltimore Magazine* and *Baltimore City Paper*. A previous collection, *Smoky Ordinary*, won the Serena McDonald Kennedy Award and was published by Snake Nation Press. She has been a fellow at the Virginia Center for the Creative Arts, the Sozopol Fiction Seminars in Bulgaria, and Le Moulin à Nef in France. She is an associate professor at Goucher College in Maryland.

Mary Jo Firth Gillett's collection, *Soluble Fish*, won the Crab Orchard Series in Poetry First Book Award. She's also published four award-winning chapbooks, most recently *Dance Like a Flame*. Her poems have appeared in *The Harvard Review*, *The Southern Review*, *Third Coast*, *Michigan Quarterly Review*, *Green Mountains Review*, *The Gettysburg Review*, *Salamander*, and other journals. She's received the N.Y. Open Voice Poetry Award and a Kresge Fellowship.

Mac Greene has never seen *The Walking Dead*, unless you mean the ones all around us. He has been writing for ten years, just to chase away the Frights, because real life is scarier than fiction. In his day job, he is a Clinical Psychologist, which means he talks about trauma and tragedy, hour after hour, year after year. He specializes in teenagers because they live closer to the bone, and Queer kids because they need people who care. The real lesson is that hope and love will beat out fear and despair.

Elizabeth Hazen is a poet and essayist whose work has appeared in *Best American Poetry 2013*, *Southwest Review*, *The Threepenny Review*, *The Normal School*, and other journals. She teaches English at Calvert School in Baltimore, Maryland. *Chaos Theories* is her first book.

Lynn Marie Houston holds a Ph.D. in English from Arizona State and is currently completing her M.F.A. at Southern Connecticut State University. She is the author of *The Clever Dream of Man* (Aldrich Press), a book of poetry about her relationships with men which won 1st place in the 2016 Connecticut Press's statewide literary competition and then went on to take 2nd place in the nationwide contest of the National Federation of Press Women. Her creative nonfiction has appeared in *Word Riot*, *Squalorly*, *Bluestem*, *Full Grown People*, *Cleaver*, and other journals. She has held writing residencies at the Vermont Studio Center and the Sundress Academy for the Arts. For more about her work, visit lynnmhouston.wordpress.com

Charles Jensen is the author of *Breakup/Breakdown* (Five Oaks Press, 2017) and *The First Risk*, which was a finalist for the 2010 Lambda Literary Award. His previous chapbooks include *Living Things*, which won the 2006 Frank O'Hara Chapbook Award, and *The Strange Case of Maribel Dixon*. A past recipient of an Artist's Project Grant from the Arizona Commission on the Arts, his poetry has appeared in *American Poetry Review*, *Bloom*, *Columbia Poetry Review*, *Copper Nickel*, *Field*, *The Journal*, *New England Review*, and *Prairie Schooner*. He lives in Los Angeles.

Adrian C. Louis grew up in northern Nevada and is an enrolled member of the Lovelock Paiute Tribe. From 1984-97, Louis taught at Oglala Lakota College on the Pine Ridge Reservation of South Dakota. He recently retired as Professor of English at Minnesota State University in Marshall. His most recent book of poems is *Random Exorcisms* (Pleiades Press, 2016). More info at Adrian-C-Louis.com.

Peter E. Murphy was born in Wales and grew up in New York City, where he operated heavy equipment, managed a nightclub and drove a cab. He is the author of *Stubborn Child*, a finalist for the 2006 Paterson Poetry Prize, *Challenges for the Delusional*, and four chapbooks of poetry. He is the founder of Murphy Writing of Stockton University which sponsors the annual Winter Poetry & Prose Getaway and other programs for poets, writers and teachers in the U.S. and abroad.

Jennifer Perrine is the author of *No Confession, No Mass*, winner of the 2016 Audre Lorde Award for Lesbian Poetry and the 2014 Prairie Schooner Book Prize in Poetry; *In the Human Zoo*, recipient of the 2010 Agha Shahid Ali Poetry Prize; and *The Body Is No Machine*, winner of the 2008 Devil's Kitchen Reading Award in Poetry. For more information, visit www.jenniferperrine.org.

Susan Allspaw Pomeroy defies writerly expectations by marrying the life of a poetess with that of a scientist/techie. Not surprisingly, the poet takes precedence. She is the author of *Little Oblivion*, a poetry collection that gives voice to Antarctica's stark, impressionable landscape—which came out of her voyage to the South Pole during her 15-year tenure with the US Antarctic Program. Though equipped with the requisite English and Creative Writing degrees, she's also a security program manager for an email service provider. Additionally, she's been a visiting writer for universities in Denver.

Stephen Roger Powers started writing poetry almost twenty years ago to pass time in the middle of the night when he was too energized to sleep after coming off the stage in comedy clubs around the Midwest. He is the author of *The Follower's Tale* and *Hello, Stephen*, both published by Salmon Poetry. He hasn't done stand-up in a long time, but every once in a while he finds avenues for the performer he was born to be. He was an extra in *Joyful Noise* with Queen Latifah and Dolly Parton, and he can be seen if you know just where to look.

Aurelius Raines II writes and lives in Chicago with his wife, Pam, and his two sons. He likes to write about the human condition and is obsessed with entropy. He is the author of two books of poetry, *I've Got A Hole In My Lip. . .* and *Love Songs To The Revolution.* He has been published in the online journal *Timbooktu*. When he is not writing, he teaches science to middle-schoolers by showing them how to use biology, chemistry and physics to survive the end of civilization. Teaching middle-school tends to make Aurelius believe that the end is nigh.

Rikki Santer's work has appeared in numerous publications including *Ms. Magazine*, *Poetry East*, *Margie*, *Crab Orchard Review*, *Grimm* and *The Main Street Rag*. She is the author of several poetry collections: *Front Nine*, *Kahiki Redux*, *Clothesline Logic* (a finalist in Pudding House's national chapbook competition), *Fishing for Rabbits* (Kattywompus Press), and *The Syntax of Trouble* (forthcoming from NightBallet Press). She lives in Columbus, Ohio where she teaches literature, writing, and film studies at a public high school. For more information, visit www.rikkisanter.com.

Carrie Shipers' poems have appeared in *Alaska Quarterly Review*, *Crab Orchard Review*, *Hayden's Ferry Review*, *New England Review*, *North American Review*, *Prairie Schooner*, and *The Southern Review*, among other journals. She is the author of two chapbooks and three full-length collections, *Ordinary Mourning* (ABZ Press, 2010), *Cause for Concern* (Able Muse Press, 2015), and *Family Resemblances* (University of New Mexico Press, 2016).

Steffi Shook is a Ph.D. student studying media and focusing on video games, gender and sexuality, and marginalized media production. She has previously been published in *Poetry Quarterly*, *The Flagler Review*, and *Star 82 Review*.

J.D. Smith's fourth collection of poetry, *The Killing Tree*, is being published in 2016. His other books include the humor collection *Notes of a Tourist on Planet Earth* (2013), the essay collection *Dowsing and Science* (2011), and the children's picture book *The Best Mariachi in the World* (2008). He has also written a poem on the *chupacabra*. Smith lives with his wife Paula Van Lare and their rescue animals in Washington, DC.

Jennifer Spiegel is the author of two books, *The Freak Chronicles* (a story collection) and *Love Slave* (a novel). Currently, she is at work on both a novel and a memoir-in-almost-real-time. She is also half of Snotty Literati, a book-reviewing gig with Lara Smith (onelitchick.com). Besides writing, Jennifer teaches and does the mom-thing. When she watches TV with her husband, she pretends it's an academic endeavor.

Jamie Sullivan has taught writing and literature at a small college in South Dakota for a long time. He has published poetry in many literary journals. He likes to hike in wild areas to hunt for snakes, fossils, and natural curiosities and has in the process found more than one poem.

Dawn Tefft's poems appear in *Fence*, *Denver Quarterly*, and *Witness*, among other journals. Her chapbooks include *Fist* (Dancing Girl Press), *The Walking Dead: A Lyric* (Finishing Line Press), and *Field Trip to My Mother and Other Exotic Locations* (*Mudlark*). Her nonfiction has been published in *PopMatters*, *Truthout*, and Woodland Pattern's blog. She holds a Ph.D. in Creative Writing from University of Wisconsin-Milwaukee and works as a higher ed union organizer.

Richard K. Weems (www.weemsnet.net) most recently published *Stark Raving Blue*, a collection of flash fiction and essays. Also, an expanded edition of his first collection, *Anything He Wants*. Zombie stories have appeared recently in *Passages North* and *Festival Writer* and forthcoming in *Del Sol SFF*. This essay comes from a current project, tentatively titled *Everything I Need to Know I Learned from Zombie Movies*. He lives and teaches in New Jersey.